TRAINING IN MISSION

ST COLM'S COLLEGE
CHURCH OF SCOTLAND

MARJORIE STEWART, B.A.

Foreword by
BISHOP LESSLIE NEWBIGIN

THE SAINT ANDREW PRESS
EDINBURGH

© THE SAINT ANDREW PRESS 1972

Published by the Saint Andrew Press 1972
121 George Street, Edinburgh EH2 4YN

ISBN 0 7152 0219 7

Printed in Great Britain by HOWIE & SEATH LTD., Edinburgh

Foreword

THE reader who is invited today to study the story of a missionary training college may be tempted to pass it by as something peripheral to current concerns. But it would be a mistake to by-pass this book. Just because we are living at a time when all traditional concepts of mission are called in question, it is important that a study of this kind should be done.

What is quite certain is that a Church with no sense of mission is already on the way to death. However mission may have to be defined and redefined, it must remain central to the Church's preoccupation. There is an enduring tension between that concept of mission which sees it in terms of the accomplishment of God's will for the entire world, and that which thinks in terms of the call to individual men and women to break away from the world as it is in order to belong wholly to God. Yet ultimately these two concepts are necessary to each other and mission cannot be defined exclusively as one or the other. Though certain elements of the present debate are new, it is not a new thing that mission should be the subject of intense questioning and doubt.

This book is the record of patient and dedicated and courageous efforts to think out and put into practice fundamental ideas concerning the kind of training of the whole person which is needed for the Christian mission. As such it is of abiding importance for the present debate. Missionary training in the traditional sense may need radical re-thinking; but missionary training in some sense there must be. It is not enough to say that every Christian is to be a missionary.   There is a sense in which this is true, but there is also another and vital sense in which mission is the concern of a minority who are called to go out beyond existing frontiers and to penetrate into new worlds (which may be right on our doorstep) with the call of the Gospel. At a time when we are unclear about the way forward, it becomes all the more important to pay heed to the experience of the past.   I therefore commend this book to those who care about the Church's continuing faithfulness to her mission.

LESSLIE NEWBIGIN

Contents

Preface

THIS book is neither a history nor a chronological record. It is rather an account of St Colm's, the Training College of the Church of Scotland (Presbyterian), and its far-sighted, pioneering and imaginative policy in training men and women for mission in the Christian Church at home and overseas. A significant element of the curriculum is the interaction between principle and practice, between study and continuous involvement in public and neighbourhood affairs.

The material, which covers the years between 1894 and 1970, has been contributed by several generations of staff and students, and assembled by a group of those who know and love the College. In this respect, grateful acknowledgement is also made to two earlier publications, *Memories of Fifty Years 1894–1944*, and *The Three Windows* by Olive Wyon. This is the story of men and women living in a community who are given time for preparation and self-discovery before going forth as messengers of the Word.

A*

CHAPTER ONE

A College is Established

IN October 1894, at 31 George Square, Edinburgh, the Missionary Training Institute of the Free Church of Scotland opened its doors to the first three women students who had offered themselves as candidates for Mission work overseas. The Women's Foreign Mission Committee had realised the necessity for a period of training before any woman was sent abroad to undertake the demanding assignments by which she was confronted in the last two decades of the nineteenth century. Miss Rainy and Mrs Cleghorn initiated the project in June 1894, and by October the premises were ready and the Principal had been found.

Annie Hunter Small was the ideal choice for this pioneer work. She was born in 1857 at Redding, near Falkirk, of comfortable, middle-class folk of Lowland origin, with an enlivening element of Irish thrown in. 'My kindred,' she wrote, 'were plain, working folk of the high Scottish tradition, hard workers, but readers too, and thinkers, patriots with no sentiment about it, theologians and Church folk, above all God-fearing men and women.' Her father, the Reverend John Small, became a missionary in Western India and his wife and three small children followed him there, in a voyage that took almost four months. Annie was six years old when they arrived and from then until she was ten she learned to know and love India. After schooling

at Walthamstow (now Walthamstow Hall, Sevenoaks), she
returned to India as a missionary at the age of eighteen.
'I started my Indian career,' she wrote, 'with one piece
of uncommon equipment. . . . I had carried on from
childhood a passionate love for India and her people. As
between Great Britain and India in their mutual relationship
I was on the side of India every time.' She knew the
degradation, cruelty and superstition to be found in India,
but 'I criticised hotly our British restlessness, acquisitive-
ness, self-assertion; our talk of commerce while intending
conquest, our attempts to gloss over our not very admirable
ambitions with what seemed to my youthful partisanship a
hypocritical profession for the good of India.'

This official lack of understanding caused Annie Small
much suffering, though she added: 'It is, I hope, unnecessary
to mention that our opinions were kept to ourselves.
Absolute public loyalty to the Government was both law
and practice with us.' She learned through bitter experience
the necessity for missionaries to be loyal to one another;
mostly she learned from her father, from his wisdom, his
deep faith, his courtesy, his humour. Gradually she found
her own ways to commend the Gospel. 'Whenever my
visits were periodic, in school or home, instead of the
Bible lesson which wound up the hours of work, I read
from the Gospels, making no comment whatever except
the necessary circumstantial explanations. On and on I
read, deliberately, watchfully, until interrupted by remark
or question. The interruption was my opportunity. . . .
The story of the Cross—rarely read—was almost invariably
heard in silence. There lay one's chance.' Out of this
and other experiments she felt she was learning 'the first
principle of missionary access: first, that the Gospel we
carry can be contained in no stereotyped form, but must
and can be spoken to each soul and to each group according

to previous conceptions of God, and to the newly awakening desire or discovered need; and secondly, that no vision of God, no individual or group desire or need can be present which Jesus Christ, who is himself our Gospel, cannot quite literally satisfy. When all is said, and very much can be said, about the world's terrible plight, his is still the first and his the last word in the matter of its relief.'

Annie Small had insight, as of one adopted, into the thought and tradition of the true Oriental. Her book, *Yeshudas, a Bond-Servant of Jesus*, was written as a gift for her father and ran into three editions. It expresses her sensitive awareness of the hunger of the Seeker, her deep respect for the age-long search of the Indian Contemplative, the Brahman who waits before God, 'the purest Brahman type, intellect and grace predominating rather than strength'. It is the story of a young Indian searching with single-minded dedication for confirmation of vague news he had heard of an Incarnate One, the Healer, and of his acceptance of the Christian faith through direct contact of the human spirit with the Creator-Father—'the loving heart in touch with its Lord's own love'. Appreciating the 'patient apprenticeship to thought and meditation' of Eastern lands, Miss Small concludes in her preface: 'There are those who believe that whole regions of the life and character and teaching and significance of Jesus Christ are still unexplored, and that probably they will remain so until the peoples of Asia, and especially of India, shall have taken the Gospels into their own hands and shall have studied and expounded them.'

After sixteen years of service in Western India, Annie Small fell ill and was ordered home, never to return to missionary service, but these years were the ideal preparation for the work that lay before her.

During the two years she spent in recovering her health

she grew to know Scotland in a new way. She saw her own people with a fresh and clear insight.

For the first time, too, she came to know about the life of the Church in Scotland. 'I was disappointed and disillusioned in almost every direction. Scottish Church life seemed isolated from that of greater Christendom. Denominationalism almost amounting to jealousy existed even between members of one Presbyterian family.' The form of Service did not appeal to her, she felt that the prominence given to the sermon destroyed the balance of worship, and she was distressed by the fact that the whole matter of public worship seemed to be approached solely from the intellectual angle. 'Our knowledge of God has reached us through our brains. The "Foolishness of preaching" has become the "Fine Art of Preaching," in matter and in manner.'

She was surprised, too, at the position of women in the Church. 'In the missionary community from which I came we were a team. We aimed at a co-ordinated and balanced inter-relation of all departments of the work, guided by frequent consultation. That is, I think, the ideal of all missionary service. The condition of Church service at home, in certain aspects of it, amazed and shocked me. There were, I found, two parallel working groups in most congregations, the official and the other—mainly composed of women—which supplied the workers.'

Yet she learned to appreciate much in the Church and came to love it, just as she learned to love Edinburgh and the many fine people there. One of her new friends was Miss Rainy, sister of Principal Rainy of New College, Edinburgh, the Theological College of the Free Church. In her spacious drawing-room at 25 George Square, childhood home of Sir Walter Scott, she heard stories of the past and hopes for the future, with no idea that Miss

Rainy was already dreaming of a Missionary College for women, and that Annie Small herself should be the first Principal.

It was in October 1894, at the age of thirty-seven, that she took up the appointment of Superintendent of the Missionary Training Institute of the Free Church of Scotland. Of the three students—one Irish, one English, one Scots—enrolled in 1894 the Irish Elizabeth Carothers came to be the first name on the roll of honour, as she died of cholera in India two years later.

The following year ten students were enrolled, five from the Free Church, two from the Presbyterian Church in Ireland, one from the English Presbyterian Church, and two from Poona. They spent two and a half years in George Square; gradually the aims of missionary preparation began to take shape in worship, study, practical service and communal life.

Numbers increased, and in 1897 a larger house was taken at 16 Atholl Crescent. Miss Mary Martin had been appointed to assist Miss Small during the last year in George Square, but she had to give up through ill-health. She was succeeded by Miss Kate Hammer, a former student, who had taken her Master of Arts degree at Trinity College, Dublin, and had studied at Newnham College, Cambridge. She was particularly interested in education. She served the College for thirty-three years, and from the beginning took charge of Home Mission work, especially in Sunday school, girls' clubs, visiting and women's meetings. By 1900 she was giving lectures in the Theory of Education and the students were visiting local day schools. Her interest in the Montessori method led her to apply new insights in her teaching and she became a member of the Kindergarten Circle in Edinburgh. Her sister, a qualified Kindergarten teacher, helped with lectures at the Institute for one term while Miss Hammer took the Higher Certificate of the National Froebel Union.

Following this, in 1901, a Kindergarten was opened in the Training Institute which met for two hours each morning in the dining-room. This imaginative form of preparation for missionary work was intended to give graduate teachers some experience of new Primary School methods. To Home Mission students it introduced ideas for handwork, story-telling and music as well as providing practical observation in child psychology alongside their lectures. Later, nurses in training for overseas work found it valuable for their understanding of small children.

During the ten years in Atholl Crescent Miss Small reported that they had had candidates from every British Missionary Society, and that other students had come from Germany, Switzerland, France, Denmark and Norway. It was realised that a building specially designed for the growing numbers and the expanding work of the Institute was required, and plans were made to find a site and to raise funds. The United Free Church—as it had become since the Union in 1900 between the Free Church and the United Presbyterian Church—supported the scheme, but the money actually came from individuals, congregations and groups of former students. Staff and students then at College made themselves responsible for raising the money required for a Prayer Room and a Rest Room.

A site was obtained in Inverleith Terrace, overlooking the Royal Botanic Gardens and with a magnificent view of the city sky-line from Arthur's Seat to the Castle. The architect, Mr Gordon Wright, worked with Miss Small to realise her dreams. The cornerstone of the building was the Chapel. There were individual study-bedrooms, and though they were tiny they provided opportunity for private withdrawal within community life.

The name *Women's Missionary College* of the United Free Church was given to it and the foundation stone was laid on October 17th 1908, most fittingly by the then Moderator of the General Assembly, the great pioneer missionary, Dr Laws of Livingstonia. In the cavity under the stone were placed certain documents by the Committee, and, as Miss Small herself says: 'a sealed packet from ourselves containing an attar-of-roses phial, the nearest symbol we could find of the alabaster cruse of Mary, into which we poured earth from the grave of St Columba and sand from Martyr's Bay, Iona, symbolising our desire to be within the succession of the ancient missionary Church of our land; we added copies of our various literature, a group photograph and the signatures of the staff and students of the time.'

In May 1909 the house was occupied for a short summer term.

The year 1910 was memorable for Edinburgh and for the future of the Church, as the first World Missionary Conference was held in the Assembly Hall. A student of that year recalled: 'It brought together some thousands of missionaries of all nations. Every day for four weeks meetings were held in the Assembly Hall, the Usher Hall and other smaller meeting places.' Mr J. H. Oldham was the head of a large and enthusiastic staff; he was a friend of Miss Small. She invited a number of special guests to stay at the College, among them men now known to us as President Harada of Japan, Bishop Azariah of India, the Reverend Thang Kang Sangma of Assam, Professor Tong Tsing-on of China, Bishop Bashford of Peking, Miss Ruth Rouse, and Dr Nicol Macnicol of India whose daughter was to become Principal of the College thirty years later.

Students were assigned to look after these visitors and this brought them into close contact with people whom they would not otherwise have met.

On one occasion a choir failed to turn up at an Assembly
Hall meeting.   An urgent call to the College brought a
dozen students hurrying to the Hall, deciding on the way
what they should sing.   Miss Small had taught them Indian
and Chinese hymns, and these they sang from the front
seats in the gallery.

A daily buffet lunch in the College dining-room brought
together many well-known guests, a unique experience for
the College group.

As a pioneer in missionary training, Miss Small, who had
been a member of the Conference Preparatory Committee,
was asked to prepare a paper describing her training policy.
Through this she became involved in the development of
other training colleges for Mission work; during the
following years she was glad to welcome to St Colm's
several Principals as they came to gain experience before
taking up their work.

By 1913 the International Intercession Union of Women's
Missionary Colleges had started, linking in prayer on the
first Sunday of each month the staff and students of seventeen
colleges or hostels in the United Kingdom, Germany,
Switzerland and Norway.

It is significant that the Edinburgh Conference Report
states (p. 270) that the missionary should be trained in the
art of teaching, 'an art which has as one of its first principles,
the finding of the true point of contact with the hearer'.

In memory of 'Edinburgh 1910' beautiful silver Communion vessels were presented to the College by Dr Oldham.

The work in College grew vigorously.   During the first
nineteen years 245 students had received preparation for
missionary service.   Candidates came not only from the
Church in Scotland and the Irish Presbyterian Church, but
also from the Anglican, Baptist, Congregational and Presbyterian churches in the British Isles, as well as from the

Basel Mission in Switzerland, and from other continental countries.

Missionary training included preparation for service in every department of the Church's activity. A survey made in 1914 of former student employment showed that over ninety of them were variously engaged—in the service of the United Free Church in the Highlands, in town and country Home Mission districts, amongst the Jews, and with each of the Church's Foreign Mission Councils in India, China and Africa. In addition, a number of old students, prevented from taking up work away from home, found outlet in the varied activities of a congregation.

As applications were being received for students to fill these diverse posts, it was considered wise to invite representation from the Jewish Mission, the Ladies' Highland Association and the Girls' Auxiliary. On the College Committee there were already representatives of those Committees of the Church who sent candidates there for training.

In its basic principles, in its purposeful development, the College was the reflection of Miss Small. The outstanding feature in its curriculum was its integrated, organic programme planned round the vital core of worship, study and personal involvement in practical field work. In Miss Small's words: 'The calling of a missionary of Jesus Christ, whether Home or Foreign, is to a *life*, not to a mere life-work or profession; not only so, but it is to a life highly specialised. She preaches, teaches, heals, and those duties must be truly and finely done; done too with a delicate understanding of their ultimate significance; for this reason, that they are the exterior expression of something interior and immeasurably great.'

It was essentially through the life of the community, watchful for the Word, so often spoken yet seldom recognised, that students grew in living relationship with Christ, maturing through self-discovery, responsibility and challenging involvement, both inside and outside the walls of the College.

Study was no mere academic exercise; it was the response to imperative need for wisdom in daily relationships and performance of duties. It was exploration in the realm of what has so often become the dead Word, killed by weary tradition, but ready to burst into flame as its living quality is encountered by the Bible Study group struggling towards the Light within. Miss Small fought against fear-ridden limitation, bursting out to an older group of women fearful of the modern approach: 'It seems to me, my dears, that your Bible consists of three beasts—a Serpent, an Ass, and a Whale.'

The curriculum in all its variety was a continuous discovery of the world's riches, of priorities, of new methods for communication, of human nature, of relationships. Students in group work were startled by new concepts that sprang from unheeded depths; thought took shape and lived. Lectures resolved themselves into seminars and discussion in which free participation released creative thought, leading to effective team work in the practical sphere.

Practical work in the community was thus the natural outcome of worship and study. The task of intercession concerned not only the women and children in the fellowships and clubs in which the students served, but also the communities around the world in which lay their future service. The women's meetings proved an opportunity to make explicit the personal discoveries made in College; the children's play groups, Sunday school, clubs and camps were life at its most friendly, its most provocative, its most unpredictable—exhausting perhaps, but lit with reality and exciting potential. There was no disturbing dichotomy between classroom and practical work; theory was checked in practice, followed by careful evaluation; new knowledge was swiftly directed to the service of human concerns. The secular was the vehicle of the sacred, and both were discovered as holy. Students came to realise the value of persons, not as objects to be manipulated, as cases to be helped, but as invaluable opportunity for relationship in love.

Within the novel experience of community life students learned something of what it meant to be a real person, not an easy achievement, especially when inspired by a sense of mission. William Penn said of George Fox: 'He was an original, no man's copy.' Through encounter with people and events in the confines of College life discovery of one's personal 'original' was sometimes a devastating but salutary enlightenment.

Growth was a quiet, deepening experience perhaps realised only after a period of years by a St Colm's student. It came in many ways. There was the expansion of boundaries through the daily encounter with varied nationalities in the student group; during the first twenty years students came from England, Ireland, Wales, Germany, Switzerland, France, Sweden, Norway, Denmark and India, from at least twelve branches of the Christian Church—bewildering when united in one small community. Visitors came from many areas of the world and told of customs, traditions and changes in far-off peoples, describing the work in which they themselves were active. The College was involved in national and international events.

There were evenings in the Common Room when many were introduced to a new perception of art, literature, music, drama. There were the Friday 'At Homes' and other occasions when students practised the skill of hostessing.

The threefold cord which continues to bind the widely scattered membership of the College goes back to a discussion on the first Sunday afternoon when Miss Small with her few students decided three basic commitments. (*a*) The college motto, 'He calleth his own by name, he leadeth them out, they follow him, for they know his voice.' (*b*) The Law of Loyalty, 'To think, to speak, to act according to the spirit of Christian sonship and brotherhood: "As I have loved you, that ye also love one another".' This enduring directive has been a continuous challenge and though there are inevitable failures, the Spirit triumphs. (*c*) Intercession for members of the new community and their work, preserved weekly down the years as numbers grew—'Let us remember before God . . .', the approach of a group not presuming to dictate, a group at one in sympathy and imagination with the person for whom they pray, united within the experience of God.

As early as 1911 Miss Small intimated to the College Committee that it was her intention to resign within a year or two. Pressure of work within the College and response to many demands from outside brought the realisation that it was time to look for a successor, and in July 1913 her appointment, by her own decision, came to an end.

Miss Mackenzie wrote of her some years later:

> 'Outstanding in my impression of Miss Small's influence upon me has always been the sense of the quality of her missionary spirit. It gave her power to attract mind as well as heart. It opened up the imagination to a fresh eagerness of desire to live and serve. It was sane and far-sighted to a degree. As the years pass and missionary life adapts itself to the demands of ever-changing conditions, I believe that Miss Small's conception of a missionary will be found to have in it the eternal element of truth which must remain.'

This was confirmed by staff and students in 1958: 'Each year in College is different, yet the basic pattern remains.

This was brought home to us again as we studied Miss Small's work, in preparation for our Assembly Exhibition. There we used the same themes to illustrate the life of Miss Small and the life of the College this year—Faith, Worship, the Church, the World, Communication and our life together.'

CHAPTER TWO

Continued Exploration

Miss Florence Mackenzie succeeded Miss Small in 1913 at the age of twenty-nine and continued to implement her policy as well as to expand diverse opportunities for practical work. Born in India and brought up in Edinburgh where she attended the University for two years before going to Girton College, Cambridge, she was thoroughly at home in the life of the Church and well-versed in its work at home and overseas. She had strong links with the Student Christian Movement of that day and on her return to Edinburgh in 1906 she retained her interest in student life. In 1908 as Central President of the Girls' Auxiliary of the United Free Church she travelled throughout Scotland gaining a personal knowlege of the life of the Church as a whole.

Miss Wyld, who joined the staff in 1910, stayed until 1916. She had read widely in Sociology and Economics under the auspices of the Edinburgh Association for the University Education of Women. She laid the foundations of Home Mission Studies, with special reference to the development of the Church Sister movement.

Development in Kindergarten Work

The Kindergarten, having been closed for a period following the move to Inverleith Terrace, was re-opened in 1915 and was held in the College dining-room. Kindergarten work was again included in the curriculum. Later a sunny class-room with windows opening to the lower garden was gifted by the parents of two of the first Kindergarten pupils, the father being the celebrated paediatric specialist, Dr John Thomson.

Miss Hammer had introduced the Montessori method with its teaching apparatus, thus emphasising the importance of sense training and activity in learning. Miss Harris, who succeeded Miss Hammer as director of the Kindergarten in 1931, experimented further on Froebel lines and adapted for young children the Dewey Project Method, introducing graded programmes of work which the children carried out individually, while combining for group work to supplement the learning process. This method encouraged initiative, responsibility and concentration. Students were often asked to sit unobtrusively in the window seats and do nothing but *watch* the children at work, as they consulted their programmes and went purposively to cupboards for 'yellow boxes' (Number), 'blue boxes' (Reading), for puzzles and sense training apparatus. Such observation gave understanding of the individual child, but the experience of just watching was for some students quite a new discipline. One student who, with a whistle, had by drill method controlled a class of seventy in a former school, found in a group of fifteen to twenty eager youngsters engaged in their own ploys a new appreciation of the individual approach towards personal relationship and understanding.

In 1931 Miss Catherine Fairley was appointed as assistant; and, as older children came in, she made apparatus required for the individual programmes of work. When Miss Fairley left in 1938, Miss Alison Stewart was appointed in her place. As Miss Harris's commitments in general training and lecturing increased, Miss Stewart gradually took over full responsibility for both the Kindergarten and the training class for students involved. In the forties visitors from nursery schools and Moray House Training College came as observers, and students from the Edinburgh College of Domestic Science who were doing their pre-Nursing training came to gain some understanding of small children and to see simple apparatus and handwork which might be of help with sick children. With about fifteen to twenty children from four to seven years old, there was a hub of activity in the lower reaches of St Colm's; and students labouring over academic work upstairs were often cheered by young voices at play on the tennis court or busy with handwork in the garden. College chapel was not a regular place for Bible Story time, but the children loved going upstairs and tip-toeing along the corridor past the lecture room so as not to disturb 'the ladies'. They were eager-eyed as they heard the meaning of the stained glass window, as they gathered round the organ to sing, as they listened to a vivid story.

The Kindergarten held a real place in the neighbourhood and children were often enrolled from birth. Parents appreciated the links with St Colm's and many were aware of its purpose of mission; they valued the knowledge that they and their children were part of the fellowship of concern and care. By 1955, however, it was becoming increasingly difficult to fit all subjects into a more academic curriculum. The entry of men into the student body put pressure on space and the large school room was needed for lectures in order to set free the Library for its true function. So to the sorrow of parents and children the Kindergarten was closed.

Miss A. E. Marjorie Moinet, M.A., born in London of Scots Presbyterian parentage, joined the College staff for the session 1919–1920 while on furlough from India, and in 1924 accepted a permanent appointment to lecture in

Church History and to direct the Home Mission and Social Studies as well as the Area Studies connected with India. Later she became Vice-Principal, and in 1939, after a year as Acting Principal, she retired.

While at Somerville College, Oxford, in her student days she had become interested in the newly-founded Missionary Settlement for University Women in Bombay; for a time she undertook the London Secretaryship and then for two tours served at the Settlement, at the same time lecturing on History at the Elphinstone College, Bombay. Her previous experience of the work of a Poor Law Guardian in Kent proved a useful background for investigating living conditions amongst the industrial population of Bombay.

Under the guidance of Miss J. Currie, Miss E. Craig and then Miss Moinet, training for Home Mission work developed in such a way that the College was enabled to explore increasing possibilities for a Church Sister Course; by the time of the 1929 Union of the United Free Church and Church of Scotland the Home Mission course was recognised by the Assembly as the training for Church Sister work. Miss Moinet played a large part in the development of the Church Sister concept in the United Free Church during the pre-union period, and subsequently in the process leading to the uniting of Church Sisters and Deaconesses in the Church of Scotland. Her concern continued unbroken after her retirement, for while being a member of the College staff she had served on the Women's Home Mission Committee and to this she was eventually co-opted as a Life Member. In 1961 when this Committee, in conjunction with the Social Studies Department of the University of Glasgow, instituted a one-year course of theoretical and practical studies for Home Mission students, she gave the plan her enthusiastic support.

Miss Moinet continuously emphasised the necessity for

students receiving practical, supervised training in circumstances similar to those in which they would be working.
Her gift of humour could often lighten a difficult assignment
for a worried student.   Many former students pay tribute
to her influence in their life and work.   Her own life was
based on an unshakable faith and trust in God, on the
necessity of an ordered daily life rooted in prayer.   This
she was able to communicate, and while there may have
been some who did not accept easily the discipline which
she commended they found her own example to be their
strongest encouragement.

An Old Students' Association was formed in 1907 and
local groups were gradually set up in the main centres such
as Edinburgh, Glasgow, London and Belfast, as well as in
countries overseas; the link was maintained through the
annual *House Guild Letter*.

The student body came to include more graduates and
trained personnel as the needs of the mission field demanded
professional and technical qualifications of every kind.
Candidates expressed vigorous interest in the problems of
social justice and manifested a questioning approach in all
sections of study.

Miss Mackenzie saw training as a preparation for the
growing complexity of missionary life, particularly in
relation to both the social and religious outlook of another
race and the whole political situation at home and abroad
with its assertiveness, tempered by hope.   She challenged
students to define the place of the missionary at that time—
politically, socially, and within the Christian Church.   One
field worker had said: 'There is no end of room for people
who can play second fiddle *well*.'   Miss Mackenzie with the
students wrestled over thinking out afresh what was the
heart of the Christian message and how it could be expressed
so as to release local confidence and initiative.

Knowing how impossible it is to enter into relationship with those of another culture without a command of the language, Miss Mackenzie enlisted the aid of the School of Oriental and African Studies, London, and introduced the teaching of phonetics as a basis for language study whether in India, Africa or any other field.   Women candidates from St Colm's were commended for this high priority placed on language.

The Conference of the International Missionary Council took place in 1921 at Lake Mohonk, U.S.A.   Miss Mackenzie attended as a representative of the British Conference of Missionary Societies.   The emphasis lay on the developing pattern of Education in Africa, a subject made vital by the presence of Dr Aggrey of Achimota College.   He and Miss Mackenzie had much in common and became good friends.   She describes him as 'a tall figure, ebony black, standing like a strong oak, moving about very little lest he disturb the white sections of the delegation by his black face.'

Miss Mackenzie also promoted study on China and took much trouble with the Field Weeks which had for long been held in College, constituting a thorough submersion of the students in the ethos of the country concerned.   The Reverend F. W. S. O'Neill of Ireland was one of the frequent resources on China.   The students recorded of him that he lectured them by day, discussed theology by night, and talked politics at breakfast.   Miss Mackenzie had a happy knack of making these varied speakers feel at home as well as extracting full measure from their stored knowledge.   In the early years of Field Weeks students not only deepened their knowledge of India but also came to know China and Africa, which to many were little more than names on a map.

Work during the 1930's was dominated by the achievement

of the Union of the Church of Scotland and the United Free
Church of Scotland.   The signing of the Act of Union,
which was preceded by a morning service in St Giles'
Cathedral, took place on 2nd October 1929.

A development of women's work, parallel to that of the
United Free Church, had been going on since 1887 in the
Church of Scotland.   At the General Assembly of 1869 a
Committee had been appointed to consider how to promote
evangelistic effort, especially through voluntary Christian
service in co-operation with the Ministry.   One outcome
of this was the formation of the Woman's Guild in 1887;
another was the acceptance of a scheme in the same year to
revive the Order of Deaconessses on a scriptural basis and
as a recognised branch of Church organisation.   Similar
revivals had been taking place in Germany and through the
Anglican Church.   Pastor Fliedner was the pioneer in
Germany, opening the first Kaiserwerth Deaconess House
in 1833, while the Anglican Church instituted their Order
of Deaconesses some thirty years later.

In Scotland, under the stirring leadership of Professor
Archibald Hamilton Charteris, who had visited Deaconess
houses and Home Mission centres on the Continent and in
England, a centre was set up in November 1887, in Mayfield
Gardens, Edinburgh, to conduct Deaconess training for
Church work at home and abroad.   It opened with a
temporary Head until Miss Alice Maxwell took charge six
months later.   In time premises were found at Numbers
27 and 28 George Square; the work was controlled by the
Deaconess Board responsible to the Christian Life and Work
Committee of the Church of Scotland.

A district in the Pleasance belonging to the old Parish
Church of St Cuthbert's was entrusted to Deaconess House
for the practical training of workers, and for mission work
the St Ninian's Halls were built in 1891.   In 1894 the

Deaconess Hospital was opened and in 1911 the Charteris Memorial Church was erected. These buildings localised the practical training in a definite area and were themselves tangible evidence of the Church of Scotland accepting its responsibility as a National Church.

Practical work, conducted by the students and Miss Maxwell, included a great number of services and meetings, Sunday schools, Bible classes, women's meetings, children's and young people's organisations. Visiting took place constantly in the dark overcrowded tenements where drunkenness was common. There was a constant round of activities, especially at Christmas and New Year, to bring some joy to the people of the district.

Miss Maxwell was followed in her work as Head Deaconess by Miss Mary Lamond; she was succeeded by Dr Mary Dodds. It was at this stage that there took place the Union of the Church of Scotland and the United Free Church. As a result the two training centres—Deaconess House and the Women's Missionary Institute—came gradually together in a practical scheme for the joint training of women for all branches of the Church's work, a report of which was made to the General Assembly of 1934. By then the outstanding features of the scheme were that students should all reside and receive their training in the Women's Missionary College, and that the sphere for practical training should embrace the Stockbridge area and work connected with Charteris Memorial Church, as well as outside forms of service considered suitable for varied experience. Reports from the College to the General Assembly were to be made through the Committee on Christian Life and Work.

The College was thus established in the life of the re-united Church under the title: The Church of Scotland Women's Missionary College, St Colm's. The merging of the two Institutions was a difficult and delicate task made possible by the wisdom and vision of the two Principals concerned, as well as by the sympathetic guidance of the Chairman of each Board—the Reverend W. T. Cairns, D.D. of the United Free Church and the Reverend Oswald Milligan, D.D., Church of Scotland. The Reverend Charles W. G. Taylor, D.D. of St George's Church, Edinburgh, gave untiring support throughout the transition.

Miss Mackenzie was particularly well qualified to serve the College at this time of difficult transition. On her retirement in 1938 the College Report to the Assembly summed up her remarkable achievement during her twenty-five years as Principal: 'Very few epochs in history have been more testing than the past twenty-five years. During all that period Miss Mackenzie has proved herself adequate to the task of meeting a situation that was almost continually changing. In the years of war and the unrest that followed, throughout all the widening opportunities that have come with the Union of the Churches, in the changes of administration ot the affairs of the College, and in all her relations with staff and students in their corporate and devotional life, Miss Mackenzie has given full proof of the ability, sound judgment, insight into character and gift for friendship which those who appointed her to the Principalship knew she possessed.'

At the 1938 Summer Retreat there came from near and far old students to express their warm affection, admiration and gratitude. Years later a group put into words what she had meant to them:

'She gave us stability, security, just by being around. She was reserved, elusive, and yet quick to understand, to enter into individual problems with imaginative insight. There was nothing stereotyped about her outlook; she was at times bracingly unexpected in her reaction. She knew her own mind, but was always ready to listen to the thoughts, aspirations and opinions of others. A picture hung on the wall of the Missionary College portraying the original disruption of the Kirk. At the time of Union a suggestion was made by a younger person that Miss Mackenzie might have it removed. "I will," she agreed as the point struck home. She had a sharp eye for practical detail and general appearances in personal outfit and room arrangement.

'Miss Mackenzie lived in a mind-stretching, intellectual world of adventurous thought and keen judgment. Although sometimes a little paralysing she was always ready to consider varying points of view, and her dry sense of humour kept things in balance. Her Monday talks in Chapel were a challenge in depth and gave splendid nourishment. She responded vitally to the Revised Hymn Book: "Read your Hymn Book for theology," she told the students.

'There was a diffidence that made her hesitate to intrude into the affairs of those around her, but all who sought her advice were reassured by her quiet consideration, wise judgment, common sense, sympathy and vision.'

The College curriculum was enriched by the varied and regular travel of the staff. Miss Small had wide-flung experience; in 1912 Miss Hammer visited Syria and Egypt and made contacts in Jerusalem, Beirut, Tiberias, Constantinople, Budapest and Damascus; Miss Wyld visited the Western Isles of Scotland to gain knowledge of church work in the Highlands. In 1917 Miss Currie spent a summer term at the London School of Economics, living at Toynbee Hall Women's Settlement, Poplar. There she was surrounded by social problems and could take part in the lively programme of Practical Homecraft and Home Nursing, Youth work and Junior work which included Dalcroze Rhythmic Gymnastics. Older women's groups held vigorous

B

discussion on Social Reforms; Reformers and Socialists thrashed out policy on burning questions of the day—reform of women's work in industry, housing, a People's Theatre. The key-word was reconstruction. In 1921 Miss Mackenzie while attending the Lake Mohonk meeting of the International Missionary Council visited the Negro College at Tuskegee, Alabama, to study their plan of education. In 1923 she went to India to visit mission stations; her health prevented her from going on to China.

In 1927 Miss Hammer went to Belgium to attend a conference on Africa, then visited Algeria and Tunisia. In 1929 Miss Mackenzie visited the Gold Coast and Calabar in Nigeria, while Miss Moinet went to Palestine and Bulgaria and later to India. Miss Mackenzie came back with a warning against the danger of paternalism towards African society—she found there 'a richness of Christian discovery for which the world is waiting till Africa unfolds it'.

These few examples illustrate the continuing effort of the staff to broaden their first-hand knowledge of church work at home and overseas.

CHAPTER THREE

Flexibility and Expansion

FOLLOWING upon Miss Mackenzie's resignation there was a Munich-shadowed interlude during which Miss A. E. M. Moinet, thoroughly versed in College affairs, acted as Principal until the arrival from India of Miss Helen M. Macnicol in the autumn of 1939. Her account of the early war years in College states that outwardly there was not much change—they were not evacuated, the curriculum remained much the same, numbers at first varied little, but underneath there was the sense of uncertainty and helplessness in the face of overwhelming powers. Yet out of this increasing desolation there came to birth new convictions.

Firstly, as one country after another became involved and members of the College Fellowship passed into the silence of enemy territory or prison camp, there came new realisation of the unity that is in Christ, a bond that could not be broken by any human warfare.

Secondly, the hope that in God there was a future for mankind was expressed in a growing concern for youth, for the younger generation to whom nothing was stable and expediency was the only rule. To understand this outlook, to bridge the gulf, to present the Christian faith in terms in any way comprehensible became the primary concern of the College. This implied the necessity to make contact; valuable links were made through Staff activities. Miss Harris acted part-time as a Chaplain's Assistant with women in the Services; Miss Beth Davey attended an Emergency Training Course in Youth Work held in London and lasting for three months; students during the holidays worked in various forms of service; all brought back to College first-hand knowledge of real need during those years. As the number of mission students decreased the College housed more University students, thus keeping it in constant touch with that section of modern youth.

Thirdly, arising out of the conflict of the world, there came a new study and understanding of the Bible as the mirror of man's experience. In it were portrayed the same conflicting situations, the same agony of uncertainty, the same contradictions between the ideal and the actual, yet in and through all could be heard the Word of God speaking clearly to those who would listen—in their battles, their decisions, their defeats, their imprisonments. The drama of the Bible with its constant action and demand for active obedience was the focal point of that College decade. Perception came through the living personalities of the Old and New Testaments—Jeremiah found the answer to suffering in the potter's shop: not to break men, but to make them anew. Jonah in moaning for a world with the enemy excluded found that God also would be left out. Students portrayed a group in an occupied country by the choral speaking of the words of the fifth chapter of Lamentations—'our inheritance is turned unto strangers, our houses unto aliens'. They visualised the agony of a German Confessional pastor as they read in Psalm 13: 'Lighten mine eyes lest I sleep the sleep of death; lest mine enemy say, I have prevailed against him.'

The College felt a strong sense of urgency for Christian witness in that world of fast-moving events. Miss Macnicol writes in 1943: 'We are called upon to try new methods, to develop new lines of approach, not because the old ones have failed, but because we are rapidly entering a new world where men and women speak a different language and express themselves in new ways. The modern Kindergarten child knows all about bombers and nothing about bananas, but our alphabet is still apt to stick to B for Bananas.'

On the occasion of the College Jubilee, October 1944, she spoke of the sense of vast new mission fields opening up in all countries, the field of the unawakened church, of youth, of State-controlled areas of life, of inter-church relations, of the gulf between Christian and non-Christian. She stressed the need for missionaries with live, active conviction, able to hold their own in the midst of a pagan world. 'Fundamentally our College cannot change; its purpose remains the same—we are a missionary college, training missionaries of Jesus Christ.'

By September 1946 the College again had a full quota of students in training, many of them having matured through the struggle and tension of war conditions. A full programme of practical activities was renewed, the curriculum of integrated study and field work continued its rich course, visiting lecturers gave stimulus and variety, and the College took its place within the mission of the Church at a time of urgent needs and challenging opportunities. Students came again from the Continent and from countries overseas.

Miss Macnicol continued as Principal during the post-war years until her failing health brought about her resignation in 1951. For several years after her retirement she conducted classes on Foreign Mission Studies at her own home. A Scot, combining a Classics degree with a vigorous, analytical and humble mind, she approached the Bible with such adventurous expectancy that truth leapt to life in the study group and struck home in her Monday morning

sermon in Chapel. There was first the precise assembly of
recorded *facts*, then a still period of brooding, a struggle
towards meaning, almost always a friction flash, a declaration
of revealed truth—such was her method of preparation.
Symbolism came naturally to her; with her listening ear
she plunged beneath the literal surface and reached the
hidden message.

Her sermons, based on Bible passages, were frequently
wrought out of some current event in the College—a
student's depression over newly discovered inability to
cope, a particular tension, a weariness of the spirit, an
occasion for rejoicing—whatever the situation it was lifted
out of its personal, domestic limitations on to the level of
practical, workable ultimate truth, as is invariably the
achievement of every Bible recording. These sermons
reflect significantly the essence of the College aim—to
prepare for sensitive adaptation to new situations and to
find perpetual nourishment in waiting upon God.

Progressively immobilised by muscular dystrophy Helen
Macnicol's was a listening ministry. In College affairs her
wisdom and trustworthiness were deeply cherished; she
gave that quiet security so essential for a group in search of
intellectual and emotional stability in their new, demanding
vocation. Hers was a questing mind; in a poem called
December, she wrote:

> . . . a door I had never seen began to open—
> It stands half open now but I do not know what lies
>   beyond.
> No lighted room I know—perhaps it leads
> Beyond the walls. All I can see is dim,
> Not dark, unknown, not menacing.
> Wherever it leads I must go through—
> A door once opened cannot be ignored.

In 1951 the Board of St Colm's invited Dr Olive Wyon to become Principal of the College for three years. She had been a student under Miss Small in 1905 but had been prevented by ill-health from going abroad. She made her name especially as the translator of Emil Brunner's theological works and was closely involved in the study preparation for ecumenical conferences. In 1948 she became the first woman to receive the degree of Doctor of Divinity from a Scottish University (Aberdeen); in that same year she had returned to St Colm's staff while Miss Harris took a year's leave of absence to serve the Church in Jamaica.

The Board Minute written in 1966, at the time of her death, summarises her contribution at a particular stage in the life of the College:

'It was a time of new developments as the Foreign Mission Committee of the Church of Scotland had decided that its men candidates should have a term's missionary training in the College. For the first year the men and wives did not live in the College. One of the tasks was to integrate this small non-resident group with the larger one of women students who had inherited a long tradition of College life. Another was to develop stronger contacts with the Theological Colleges and with the Committees of the Church of Scotland. In these and in other aspects Dr Wyon's theological knowledge and ecumenical contacts were of great value. So were her personal gifts of understanding and friendship, especially to students from the Continent whose language and church background she knew. She believed that words should carry their own power to convince; consequently she read her lectures or addresses in a quiet manner that concealed the reader's personality and let the words speak for themselves.'

A student speaks of Dr Wyon's teaching ability, her dauntless spirit and her sympathy with people of all persuasions, an understanding and tolerance in depth. Her stimulating encouragement demanded a high standard in study and in the extensive range of practical work. The

Student Report of 1954 speaks of their wide variety of studies, the most popular being Dr Wyon's Pastoral Theology, in spite of its 'somewhat pride-shattering' effect. A special course was introduced on Modern Heresies, exposing amongst others both Spiritualism and Mormonism. A rousing study project took the form of a well prepared Conference on *The Church—Holy, Catholic and Apostolic*; all during the summer term students did intensive study, preparing and discussing papers for the Conference so that the climax was of a high order, gathering up much of the year's work and giving fresh insight into the mission of the Church.

Dr Wyon became a member of the Scottish Churches' Ecumenical Association and worked closely with the Ecumenical Dollarbeg Committee, an outcome of the Scottish Report on 'The Life and Work of Women in the Church'.

Dr Wyon made a valuable bequest to the College of her theological and devotional books, including her own writings and translations.

At the end of her three-year period she was succeeded as Principal in 1954 by Miss Celia Calder who had joined the staff in 1952, coming from educational work in Madras. Her enforced resignation on health grounds after one year was a sad blow to staff and students to whom her serenity and simplicity all through the year had been an inspiration.

There was, of necessity, during the fifties considerable reconstruction of the curriculum to meet the need of men students already trained to be ministers, as well as teachers, craftsmen and agriculturalists. The Reverend W. Young and the Reverend Albert Craig, each with missionary experience, served as tutors for the men's course, Mr Young during the 1952-53 session and Mr Craig until 1954. The

Reverend Frank Ryrie, an ex-missionary from Bengal, then became the first man to be appointed to the St Colm's staff. Not only did he supervise the men's course, but he lectured in Doctrine and shared in the work of the College.

Miss Jean Fraser who had been appointed to the staff in 1954 became Principal after the death of Miss Calder. Following upon parish work in the East End of London as a Church Sister of the English Presbyterian Church she had long experience of youth work with the British Council of Churches and the World Council of Churches. To the Church in Scotland she brought an ecumenical experience and understanding which was never merely doctrinaire. Her internationalism was spontaneous, personal and sensitive to changing conditions. She appreciated fully the traditions and foundation principles of the College and built accordingly.

The initial breadth of interest so marked in the early curriculum continued through the years, the staff being always ready to adapt to current thought and developing policy. Bascially the approach through Bible and Worship remained the guiding factor. Methods of study followed the pattern of informal lectures, seminars, group discovery and sharing, as well as expression through drama, visual representation and teaching practice in Sunday school, youth groups and at various church and non-church organisations.

By 1958 it was reported that a decreasing degree of differentiation had emerged in courses designed for men and women, and that diversity of outlook, experience and academic qualifications was no hindrance to achieving unity of spirit and purpose in self-preparation; mutual help and understanding came from living and working together, a splendid omen for future collaboration in the field of mission. The College was full, the Board declared itself

B*

satisfied that St Colm's had a vital contribution to make in training for the communication and commendation of the Gospel in the modern world. They spoke of the harmony of the staff under the leadership of Miss Fraser and called attention to the fact that St Colm's was the only college run by the Church of Scotland and providing courses of training for men and women entering upon full-time service in the Church. They noted that the great variety of curriculum, requiring at least three types of courses varying from one term to three years, must prove exacting for any staff. Students were sponsored by five Church of Scotland Committees and came as well from many lands in Europe and beyond. By 1963 the College was glad to welcome the first men students from Ireland. Most of the men without theological training now stayed for three terms and some of the ministers who, for one reason or another, were students for more than one term expressed their appreciation of the longer period.

Individual courses were planned in the light of the subsequent work of the student as well as his or her previous experience. In addition to two sessions at St Colm's, Home Mission students attended a one-year course run by the Social Studies Department of the University of Glasgow; Youth Committee students took some classes at the College of Education and New College as part of their training as members of Sunday school and Senior Youth staff; overseas mission students were able to take advantage of classes at the Muir Institute of Islamic Studies, and, when it was established, the Centre of Africa Studies at the University. A Field Study Week arranged for overseas students by Moray House was also an occasion for those going to overseas appointments to see Scottish life and institutions through the eyes of those from abroad, and to live alongside people of very varied backgrounds and religion.

Following upon the retirement of the Reverend Frank Ryrie, the Reverend Kenneth Mackenzie joined the staff in 1957 as Tutor in Mission and stayed until 1968 when he took up work in the parish of Old Restalrig, Edinburgh. His ten years in Central Africa, his command of languages and sympathetic knowledge of customs, his deep involvement in the local situation as well as in the struggle concerning safeguards for African interests during the Federation discussions, his leadership in Church Union negotiations—such was the first-hand experience that made so valuable his contribution to those training for church work both abroad and at home.

Convinced from his Christian standpoint that Federation was no answer to the needs of developing Africa he equipped himself with documented statistics and acquired the skills of political action to work for freedom from Federation. He believed in action at all levels—letters to Prime Ministers, Secretaries of State, Members of Parliament; anti-apartheid protest marches, public meetings and debate, and active Party membership. Discrimination in all forms he fought as an enemy of the Gospel.

It was under the combined influence of Jean Fraser and Kenneth Mackenzie that time was set aside for the study of current events—social, political and economic. The discipline of regular discussion in College gave directive to a balanced consideration of national and world events; on a few occasions there was deliberate involvement in public affairs.

For example, in March 1959 a letter was sent by staff and students to the High Commissioner for Rhodesia and Nyasaland making representation concerning the arrest and detention without trial of Mr Guy Clutton Brock and certain members of the staff of St Faith's Mission Farm, Southern Rhodesia. Letters were also sent to the appropriate authority in 1959, 1960, 1961 and 1968 concerning:

- a Constitution for Nyasaland permitting an absolute African majority in the Legislative Council;
- a referendum on the Central African Federation in the three Territories involved;
- the danger of immigration laws discriminating against coloured people;
- the plea that there be no recognition of Rhodesian independence before majority African rule.

Appreciation was expressed from the staff-student group to the British Broadcasting Corporation for films shown early in 1969 of conditions in Biafra with which country the College had always had close links through mission service.

Through earnest consideration of such problems the students learned to appreciate their responsibility towards an elected Government acting in their name, and to understand how and when to register support or protest. The duty of the citizen was seen as part of the Christian concern for the rights of others.

There was thus continuous challenge to the students to rethink their belief in terms of world affairs, to venture into uncertainty, to refuse to be checked by fear, to discipline uncritical enthusiasm; above all to try to be honest in thought and emotion, to align themselves sympathetically with the struggle for fair play at home and overseas. There was always the danger of high-sounding protest unrelated to direct action, but to some extent the remedy lay in practical work during both term and vacation in problem situations, and in contact with fellow students from disturbed areas in other continents.

Kenneth Mackenzie, when asked if he would teach Church History, replied that he would rather make it. With the students he shared his hard-won experience and wide reading, his vision, his serenity, his gaiety, his immense love of humanity, his insistence on accurate information as a basis for action. His every action was a ministry. His death in 1971 was sad news for all who knew and loved him. Many wrote describing his courage, insight, strength and tenderness. Kenneth Kaunda, a former colleague on a Church of Scotland school staff and now the President of the Republic of Zambia expressed to Mrs Mackenzie his sorrow: 'His passing away has come as a deep shock and blow to me personally and to this country he did so much to serve.'

Miss Fraser, after fifteen years at St Colm's, retired in 1969, and for the first time a male Principal, the Reverend Duncan Finlayson, was appointed to what had for twenty years been a co-educational college.

Miss Fraser was consistently and sometimes startlingly original and radical in her thought, deliberations and achievement. 'New ideas and stimulating questions—always clearly communicated', was the comment of one colleague.

She had splendid gifts to share with the College family—her wide knowledge of the student world, her vision of the Church's mission, her creative belief in the contribution of others—whether as individuals or as a struggling group —her involvement in every aspect of the life of College as well as her outreach to the affairs of the world near and far, her passionate concern for 'at-one-ment' in the Faith, above all her unhesitating commitment to life and relationship.

During a time of adjustment and change—of testing new methods in training, of quietly integrating each new group

of men in the early stages—her balanced judgment, incisive
thinking and accumulated experience were invaluable.   Her
own concept of mission is characteristic of her policy:

'The work of Christian missions has created new possibilities for State as well as Church in Africa, and this brings
home to us perhaps more than anything the fact that our
mission field is not only across the seas.   The Gospel of
Christ's love is as much involved in getting questions asked
in Parliament, in letters to the Press or B.B.C. interviews
as in our Greenside visitation.   May we learn what God
would teach us through it all.'

Inter-Church Activities

As indicated in the early history, the College was constantly
in touch with churches other than Presbyterian, particularly
through the Student Christian Movement and the common
interest in mission.   The 1910 World Mission Conference
in Edinburgh opened new channels of communication.   In
1911 representatives from St Colm's went to a United
Missionary Students School in London, attended by seventy
women students from eight missionary colleges and hostels,
and in the afternoons by thirty men from theological
colleges.   Topics included Comparative Studies in the
Doctrines of the Faith, The Social Message of the Missionary.
This gathering created a new interdenominational fellowship.
In 1914 a Summer School was held at College on The
Preparation of Missionaries, arranged by the Scottish
Continuation Committee of the 1910 World Conference.

These links increased as ecumenical interest developed.
The Week of Prayer for Christian Unity was normally kept
in College by using the specially prepared leaflets.   The
College also participated in events arranged by the Edinburgh
churches.   The Women's World Day of Prayer meant much

to many of the boarders from Africa, Europe and India who would all have been taking part in their own countries. At St Colm's men and women joined in the shortened service, variously conducted by orderlies, boarders, students and staff.

More and more opportunities opened up for consultation together; there was the Theological Student Conference at New College, Edinburgh in 1937, addressed by Professor John Macmurray and Professor John Baillie; the Student Christian Movement Conference in Birmingham in 1935. Visits were paid by staff members to the various denominational Mission Training Colleges in the Selly Oak complex; Miss Mackenzie visited Carey Hall, Kingsmead and Woodbrooke in 1916 and from then on there has been interchange which developed into regular contact during the past two decades. A representative of the St Colm's staff now attends the annual consultation of British Missionary Societies held at Selly Oak; on four occasions the two special lecturers appointed there each year from Asia and Africa were invited to conduct sessions at St Colm's. In 1967 the President of the Selly Oak Colleges visited St Colm's and met with the Board to discuss ways of co-operation. Close liaison is maintained with the Missionary Societies over policy and techniques, in April 1969 Miss Fraser and Mr Mackenzie took part in the European Consultation on Missiology held at Selly Oak, Birmingham.

The ecumenical character of the training, in line with the Church of Scotland's stated commitment, was enhanced in the sixties by the active participation of the students in the Theological Colleges Union, related to the Theological Colleges Department of the Student Christian Movement. Regular meetings were planned between students of New College, the Episcopal College (Coates Hall), the U.F. and Congregational College, and the Roman Catholic Seminary at Drygrange. A special relationship grew up with Coates Hall, similar in size to St Colm's and emphasising the same aspects of corporate life and worship. Joint seminars were held in the summer term at the conclusion of the Coates Hall examinations. Contact was also made with the Faith Mission College and with the Salvation Army.

Students went as part of their practical work to every kind of church event at home and abroad—work camps, conferences, study courses. They went to the Ecumenical Institute at Bossey, to the Kirchentag, the Danish St Lukas Stiftelsen. At home they took part in the Unity and Service project at Coventry Cathedral and served in neighbourhood work at the Notting Hill Ecumenical Centre. The Fellowship of St Andrew, founded to promote understanding of the Eastern Orthodox Church, usually held its annual conference at St Colm's. Students were introduced to the depth and magnificence of Orthodox worship, music and icons.

The International Diakonia Conference held in Edinburgh in 1966 involved Deaconesses and St Colm's staff rather than students. It led to a generous invitation to the four staff members, as representative of many interests of the Church of Scotland, to spend a week in Sweden to get to know the Church there in its parish work, its lay training, its home and overseas mission. The same journey gave an opportunity for a further week in Denmark, divided between Deaconess Houses and centres for overseas mission, and allowed Mr Mackenzie to take part in a Seminar for over a hundred African students studying in Scandinavian countries. These contacts all led to further exchange of visits by students, and were especially valuable where, as in Southern Yemen, Danish and Scottish missionaries were working together.

A vital breakthrough took place at a Theological Student Conference in 1969 held at Swanwick under the auspices of the British Council of Churches and the Student Christian

Movement, and called together in response to the frustration
and bewilderment about private prayer and public worship
that was so widely expressed by young and old.   It was
concerned with Contemporary Spirituality, under the title
'Death of the Soul'.

The wide range of opinion and reactions at this Conference
represented a microcosm of the Church in the United
Kingdom.   Differences were considered in depth, with pain
and compassion over conflict in the life of the churches,
Eastern and Western.   Informal sessions introduced
participants to the thought of Teilhard de Chardin, to
modern aspects of Roman Catholic spirituality, and to the
contribution of various other communities in the world of
today.   The occasion ended in a fine review that presented
a range of situations illustrating the theme 'The Death of
the Soul'.   It came to a climax in the dancing of 'The
Lord of the Dance', followed by a rousing Three Cheers
for God.

One hundred and sixty-eight people took part, most of
the participants were from forty-five theological colleges; a
significant percentage were Roman Catholic.   A number of
wives and fiancées were there and non-theological students
made their presence felt.   From St Colm's five students
and one member of staff attended this successfully unstructured Conference and came back to communicate effectively
a new spiritual dimension, expressed in various ways.   One
was freedom to use raw materials of worship such as music
(guitars, records, songs) or the chapel—stripped of chairs
and wall furnishings to allow for sitting on the floor and for
hanging posters.   They brought back challenging forms of
worship relevant to current practical needs, expressing a
wide koinonia stretching from Roman Catholic to Salvation
Army.   This resulted in some outstanding Acts of Worship,
especially in connection with Christian Aid Week.

During that summer term a group from St Colm's met with members of the Archdiocesan Laity Centre to study together documents of the World Council of Churches and Vatican 11 on Development, and on Worship.

One student, who was particularly concerned to have a better understanding of things ecumenical, was sent to attend a Seminar on the Worship and Theology of the Eastern Orthodox Church, held at the Ecumenical Institute, Bossey. She says:

'To be at Bossey was both to experience the hurt of our divisions and to learn to find one another as Christians across the barriers of theology, language and culture which we so easily allow to separate us. In our common task of understanding the Orthodox we discovered the necessity of setting these differences aside and going back to the very origins of the Church and the message of our Lord, seeing their basic truths afresh for ourselves. . . . Worship with the Orthodox, especially at the Easter Services in Paris, was an experience of joy and freedom. The richness in worship, particularly in the music and iconography was in strong contrast with our plainer Reformed ways. I never before realised how the greater part of our service was in danger of being only a prelude to the main item—the sermon. The Orthodox Liturgy is a movement from one event in the life of Christ to another, from one climax to the next; it demands from the worshipper a real giving of self in the use of all the faculties. At the Easter service the church at midnight was ablaze with the light of many candles and the air filled with the excitement of the worshippers. We were here to celebrate the Resurrection of our Lord—and we non-Orthodox really learned how to celebrate in worship, once we had overcome our usual staid ways. With what joy and delight one greeted another with the good news—"Christ is risen—He is risen indeed."

'Such a service might not be "with it" in the modern sense, but a group of teenagers from a difficult Church Extension area who went to the Easter Service in the Orthodox Chapel in Edinburgh said it was "great" and wished we could have something like it in our church. A thoughtful look at some of these icons might well help towards a better understanding of Pentecost, Trinity and other events in the Christian Year in a way that no verbal explanation ever will.'

The staff, each of whom represented a different aspect of the Church of Scotland's own involvement in mission, were all deeply involved in the committees and concerns of the Church. The proximity of the College to the Church offices made regular participation possible. The Principal was a member *ex officio* of the Overseas Council and Home Board, especially of their Candidates' Committees. Miss Fraser served as Secretary for the Special Committee of the Place of Women in the Church. She was also a member of the Committee on relations between the Church of England, the Episcopal Church of Scotland and the Church of Scotland. She served for a time on the Committee of the United Society for Christian Literature. Other members of staff were actively engaged in policy making in line with their own interests, for example in producing new Sunday School and Bible Class material, and sharing in revised planning by the Deaconess Board, or in the detailed work of Committees of the Overseas Council.

Within the College group of international and ecumenical outlook there were students of the conservative-evangelical approach. The diversity in expression of faith and aim, in choice of priorities, in religious experience at first shook their confidence in College teaching and made full participation difficult. On occasions, at their own request, they were given every opportunity to lead their own prayer life, and of course they were free to express their views in study groups. Differences which emerged coupled with diversity of personality led at times to tension, withdrawal and gloom, but the constant act of coming together in worship, household chores and study usually brought understanding leading to reconciliation and unity of spirit.

CHAPTER FOUR

The Curriculum as Illustrating Policy

THE Curriculum of the College expressed from the beginning the far-sighted deliberate policy of combining study with activity, of learning through practical experience, of evaluating theory by its application to challenging practice. Miss Small declared 'We feel that the training of a missionary consists in study, *and* in the translation of all study into terms of work and life. The latter is a slow process, it is accomplished unconsciously and must never be hastened.'

For over fifty years Mission had been established by the Church of Scotland in India and South Africa; men had been sent out qualified in Arts and Theology, but not otherwise prepared. No such course was available for women, nor was professional or technical training open to them. As Christianity continued to develop local ability in these overseas countries, it was realised that only specifically qualified women would be acceptable or effective, and that, in addition to their professional training teachers, nurses and others should have opportunity for an all-round preparation through study of the Scriptures, of doctrine, of educational method, of other religions and of mission. They also needed practical experience in home mission work, health measures and simple administration procedure.

The curriculum grew gradually and experimentally along these basic lines, subjects being added which were manifestly serviceable, the system aiming at sending out women with some appreciation of the manifold task to be undertaken and the conditions under which it must be accomplished. The full course extended over two years, though it was not always possible to retain students for the total period.

The work of the College fell into three main sections— Biblical, Educational and Missionary. The aim for including each subject was made clear in the 1903 programme which included the following courses:

1. The Bible and Christian Doctrine, showing the adaptation of the Christian Faith and teaching to varying conditions and suggesting methods of approach.

2. The History of Missions and Missionary Methods, comparing pre-Reformation results with the modern approach and stressing continuity in motive and impulse from the Early Church onwards.

3. Christianity and the non-Christian religions, with a view to deepening an understanding of other ways of approach to God and of providing a Christian apologetic relevant to the current situation.

4. Education, including the History of Education, Method, Psychology, as well as Moral and Religious Education. The aim was to prepare the student for participation in the educational development, both formal and informal, of the people amongst whom she would work.

5. Sociology, related particularly to principles underlying the evolution of society and the Church's responsibility towards modern social conditions. This course included practical experience in youth groups,

women's meetings, home and hospital visiting, all
followed by systematic discussion of organisation,
method and result.

There were also sessions on phonetics and language,
health and hygiene, physical recreational activities, and
industrial handwork such as basket making, dressmaking and
miscellaneous handcraft. Experience was provided in
committee procedure, account keeping, blackboard and
visual aid proficiency, and voice culture.

Arrangements were made whereby experienced missionaries came into residence for a brief period to give illustrated
lectures on the special conditions of work in their particular
field. These Area Weeks on Africa, India or China
constituted an effort to enter into the culture of these
countries through talks, music, dress, customs, personal
contact and even the sampling of food.

Under the Education section came the unusual inclusion
of a kindergarten run by the College. The syllabus of 1903
gave two specific reasons for this emphasis on the Theory
of Education and the Kindergarten Method:

'First the zenana missionary (having access to the
women's apartments) is a religious teacher, striving to
bring before the minds of her hearers aspects of truth which
may touch their wills and affect their lives. It is therefore
most necessary that she should understand something of the
laws of the mind. For example, the psychological fact that
new ideas can best obtain a permanent place in the mind
through the help of old ideas, will strengthen her sympathetic desire to find some common ground from which to
begin her teaching; while the fact that the value of a word
depends upon the associations connected with it in the mind
of the hearer, will awaken her anxiety to know how far
her meaning has been grasped, and will prevent her from

rashly concluding that there has been a wilful rejection of the truth itself when her presentment of it has not been welcomed. Secondly, the zenana missionary has generally the oversight of school work among the non-Christian population of her district. She must, therefore, be able to direct the work of the native teachers and to help them, both by example and precept, to rise out of the ruts of routine and mere verbal teaching. For this she needs a firm grasp of the principles of education.

'The Kindergarten Method, following the Froebel Syllabus, has been adopted because it best combines theory and practice into one living unity; it is most readily adapted to the various conditions of different lands; and also, in India it is compulsory in all State-aided schools. In Criticism Classes, Discussions and Conferences, opportunities are given for informal talks on education from the Foreign Mission standpoint. Practice in Teaching is obtained in Creche, Kindergarten and Transition Classes, and Infant Class. There the student has the opportunity of child study on her own account, and of seeing how the theories set before her in class are daily verifying themselves in the all-round development of natural, happy children.'

'Conferences'

Miss Small's policy was to encourage students to think for themselves and then to express their thoughts with clarity and conviction. One method was described as a 'Conference'; this approximated to what is now known as a Seminar. A lecture on a subject would be followed by individual study which then led on to a properly constituted Conference. Two students were given a research assignment on the chosen topic; they then presented papers to the assembled group. Questions and discussion followed, and the subject was absorbed from many angles. Topics were linked with (*a*) Bible Study, (*b*) Mission, and (*c*) Education, typical subjects being:

(*a*) Comparison of the missionary methods of Jesus and John the Baptist. Message of the Prophets to their own times and to the present day.

(*b*) The relation of Islam to Christianity. The contribution to religion of non-Christian faiths. The Christianisation of Britain. Modern religious development (Theosophy, Christian Science).

(*c*) The relation of society to the development of the complete self. Manual training in the education of children. Comparison of the methods of Froebel, Pestalozzi and Montessori. Infancy and childhood in India, China, Africa and the homeland.

A Curriculum relevant to the task of the Church

Periodical evaluation of the college curriculum was made essential by two factors:—

the changing needs of church work at home and abroad,

the previous qualification and experience of candidates for training.

The basic pattern of principle linked to practice persisted in the main, though occasionally the emphasis swung somewhat dangerously towards scholastic upgrading coupled with detached observation in the practical field, resulting in uninformed and theoretical evaluation by the uncommitted student onlooker.

During one or two periods of transition the free question and discussion method used in seminar and group study yielded to the professional lecture; creative reflection and pragmatic discovery had to struggle against traditional intellectual instruction and academic proficiency. This dilemma was rare, the functional components of the curriculum prevailed:

personal consecration and growth;

practical application of classroom teaching in worship, relationships and community service;

individual involvement in the technical skills so ably demonstrated but so elusive until tried out and proved.

Qualifications varied within the student body, where one might profess a theological or sociological competence, another might have had experience in medical or educational work or other such service to the community. It was to meet this rich variation that the staff set themselves the difficult task of planning individual timetables, so that for each the programme was complementary to that already accomplished in previous courses. Personal assessment through written work on the main subjects was found much more satisfactory than examinations.

Classes and activities were attended within the College as well as at Edinburgh University, New College and other relevant centres. A high level of attainment within the vocation of missionary service was the goal, whether in conducting a game of netball at a youth club or clarifying a theological concept unfamiliar to the student group.

Visiting Lecturers

Much of the class work was done by the resident staff, but from the first days the College has drawn upon a distinguished succession of lecturers qualified in such subjects as Biblical Studies, Christian Doctrine, Church History, Missionary Method, Comparative Religions,

Language Study, Music and the Arts. The College is deeply indebted to those men and women who conducted these courses; many came from New College, Edinburgh; others from Christ's College, Aberdeen; St Mary's College, St Andrews; Trinity College, Glasgow; Edinburgh University. Clergy of more than one denomination gave regular tuition, and missionaries of outstanding achievement made a point of visiting the College, not only at the time of Field Week study, but for constant first-hand instruction on work overseas. Those employed in the various departments of Church work gave continuous help, especially in connection with Home Mission. Various organisations sent speakers, gave demonstrations and arranged field visits; these included some statutory bodies as well as Voluntary Agencies such as the Marriage Guidance Clinic, Alcoholics Anonymous, Shelter, Rehabilitation Centres, Girl Guides and the Brigades.

Constant visitors, men and women from near and far, were an immediate link with wide areas of the world. They came to see what the College was doing, to make personal calls on the Principal and staff, to seek encouragement and advice concerning the work they were doing. Always welcome, they were set free to make any contribution that was primarily their own, whether it was to do with areas overseas or with social, cultural or theological affairs of current interest.

During Assembly Week there was a visit from the Moderator till eventually pressure of work made it impossible, and on two occasions there was a visit from the Lord High Commissioner.

In recent years the College has been visited by deaconesses from Switzerland, Sweden, Denmark, Australia and New Zealand, and student deaconesses from Uppsala have made study visits. Thus is the *Diakonia* link strengthened.

In the College records there are well-loved and famous names to be remembered, too many to be printed, but all recorded in the output of successive generations at St Colm's.

The Library

The library has been built up over the years and has been constantly revised as a working tool for staff and students. Corresponding to the needs of the curriculum the main sections are:

1. Basic subjects: the Bible; Church History up to the present day; Christian Doctrine and Apologetics; the Churches and Worship; Christian Ethics, Social and Personal.

2. Overseas Mission: Missionary policy and practice; Area Studies; Other Faiths.

3. Home Mission: Social Studies, Religious Sociology.

4. Education and Psychology; Christian Education in Home, Day School and Church, both principles and practice. Pastoralia.

Another section of the library contains literature for children, a good range of general literature, fiction and biography, as well as a remarkably 'catholic' selection about prayer and devotion, representing Christian mystics and men and women of prayer, whether Protestant, Catholic, Quaker or Orthodox, providing rich resources for students on the prayer life and the leadership of corporate prayer.

Periodicals representing publications on Christian thought today, cultural and political issues, education and area studies, help staff and students to keep up with current thought.

An excellent collection of reference material is available in folders containing pamphlets, handbooks, newspaper cuttings, study outlines and programme suggestions related to youth groups, play groups, adult groups and various active organisations; the topics include Bible Class Kits, Sunday School Schemes, Christian Education for Adults and Youth, and practical ideas for club work and group organisation, especially leadership training. In addition to this a valuable collection of teaching aids has accumulated over the years—posters, flash cards, flip charts, flannelgraphs, puppets, as well as projected aids. This is constantly added to by the ingenuity of fresh generations of students and gives excellent practice in both selection and manipulation in the presentation of a lesson.

Students are encouraged to make use of the library whether it be for research on Bible, Doctrine or Church History, or whether they are engaged in evaluating practical methods used in youth work or Sunday School and are themselves planning acceptable programmes for current assignments or future involvement. Recent organisation of the library has greatly increased its suitability for private study and continuous reference.

CHAPTER FIVE

Worship, Drama, Communication

THE Chapel is the heart of the College; there worship is
typical of its spirit of adventure and exploration, and is often
couched in contemporary language, as seeing the unchanging,
eternal God manifest in twentieth century idiom.

During the years College worship continued within the
inheritance passed on from Annie Small—a period of
individual quiet for personal prayer before proceeding to
the Chapel with its quiet, insistent summons of the Burmese
temple gong, the varied hymns from many countries, the
experience of widely different forms of worship and the
established tradition of Quiet Days and Retreats. These
things seemed clear—that prayer and worship together are
the ways in which most ordinary Christians express their
faith, that all who are training for work at home or abroad
need to get beyond their own tradition into an appreciation
of other peoples' ways, that in Chapel the College world is
placed in proper perspective within God's world—here the
God-World-Church-Ourselves relationship finds its essence
in adoration, confession, intercession, petition, thanksgiving,
dedication and silent meditation.

These essentials were worked out in the weekly pattern
of corporate worship, described here as it took place, with
modifications and adaptations, during the past two decades:

Sunday morning prayers kept the tradition of reading or
singing a Psalm from a daily scheme drawn up by Annie

Small; past or present students and staff whose birthdays fell that week were remembered by name; the work and worship of the churches represented by the student body— at home or in their present or future service—were commended to God.

Week-day morning prayers were usually conducted by staff, each having a regular day and working out his or her own theme.

Evening prayers were led by students, boarders and occasionally orderlies. A lectionary was followed which either supplemented or emphasised the parts of the Bible which were being studied. A rota of intercession was a means of remembering before God by word or silence the life of men and women at home, at work, at leisure; the life of nations and their relationship with each other; the various churches and their search for unity and understanding; the special needs encountered by students as they went about their service in the community.

Students grew in stature through their experience of leading in prayer; conventional phrases gave way to greater freedom, relevance and originality of treatment. A new tolerance for forms different from their own developed into appreciation based upon understanding; a door was opened to informed collaboration at home and abroad with Christian bodies other than their own.

Alongside the practice of prayer there was usually held in the autumn and spring terms a series of studies on the life of prayer. These took various forms, but it was found that lectures were less appreciated than the opportunity to share questions, experience and resources. The pattern of College prayers needed interpreting if people were to enter into it meaningfully; students were helped to find resources such as books and visual aids and to discover freedom in using them. Questions arose about private prayer in personal experience, especially from those influenced by a scientific outlook. The attempt to translate newspaper headings into topics for adoration, confession, petition and intercession often revealed how hard it was to make prayer specific. It was found that the people who prepared the act of worship gained most, thus making a good case for corporate preparation which, unfortunately, is time-consuming.

There was certain resistance to set forms of service, due partly to unfamiliarity, sometimes to indoctrination. This gradually yielded to acceptance through the realisation that a liturgy was a tradition of other churches, that it was helpful to those with limited English, and that it would be an alternative worthier than shoddy preparation due to lack of time. There were several sources in use—Compline, Orders compiled by the Scottish Churches House at Dunblane, by the Communities at Taizé and Iona, by Christian Aid, the German Lutheran Church, by St Colm's students, and from the far past—the Litany of Dunkeld of the late ninth century.

Music was never confined to familiar hymns. From the first years music from other times and other countries enriched the services. The hymn practice, conducted weekly, made it possible to include a splendid variety, to probe for meaning, and to constitute a time of preparation for worship. Hymns introduced from East and West, edited by Miss Small, were published as a collection which had grown from a felt need and were accompanied by the warning that without careful training it was impossible to render Oriental music with understanding. This first collection, *Missionary College Hymns*, was the basis for various recitals of Oriental music, including one given in the Assembly Hall in 1911. When the *Revised Church Hymnary* was being compiled many of the hymns were tried out in

College before the book was published in 1927. In 1963 Miss Fraser brought back from a Conference in Bangkok copies of the new *East Asian Christian Conference Hymnal*, in which half the hymns are from Asian sources. As new collections of hymns and new styles of singing were popularised, these were tried out in Chapel, one example being the production in 1966 by the Youth Department of the World Council of Churches of a workbook *Risk* for the renewal of singing, contending that the world of experience represented in hymns no longer coincides with the existential experience of our day.

Psalm tunes were taken from various sources including *The Scottish Psalter* of 1635, *English Plain Song* and the Joseph Gelineau settings.

The College session began with a Communion Service according to a Church of Scotland form and a Communion Service closed the Quiet Day of led meditation that ended each term. Students sometimes asked for more frequent communion and this request was fully discussed. The setting for the Service was occasionally changed according to the numbers taking part—it has been held in the common room, the dining-room, and in the Chapel with table and chairs moved to form an appropriate setting. Several years running the Liturgy of the Church of South India was celebrated in College. Students were encouraged to be present at celebrations of the Eucharist in other Churches.

Students of the 1942-43 course wrote to the scattered College Fellowship: 'Our keeping of the Christian Year has been a means of deepening our communion in the Church Universal. Preparation for receiving Christ at Christmas and appropriating His Sacrifice at Easter culminated in Festival Services in Chapel where, in the light of the Incarnation and the Atonement, we prayed for the world He created and redeemed. Around the Lord's Table this varied household has been conscious of its unity in Christ and of the bonds of love which hold you and ourselves together.'

The rhythm of the Church's year was observed in the choice of readings and hymns as well as by special events. For Advent: the wreath, with four candles, hymns sung by second year students before the rising bell, a specially decorated dining-room for tea, such was the contribution of the Continentals. The vexed question of the use of candles was hotly debated, many were reconciled though some protested at candles in Chapel. As no one was in College for Christmas the Advent season made significant preparation, including the Act of Worship which involved serious study of the Christmas message for today.

Lent was another tradition unfamiliar to many. Time was usually taken to interpret it as an opportunity, similar to that of Advent, of realising experience treasured by others. It fell half-way through the College year when there was an appropriate individual check on the use of time. Sometimes agreement was reached about quiet from 10 p.m. to 7 a.m., or a Lenten offering or a simpler midday meal once a week; at times decision was left to the individual. There were special forms of worship in Chapel.

On the rare occasions when in residence at Easter the College tried to make this a time of joining with the wider Church. Miss Fraser describes an exceptionally varied celebration of Easter events in 1967:

'Our Easter celebrations really started with a hilarious Irish party on St Patrick's Day, 17th March. During Holy Week we changed our normal times of evening prayers and had compline at 10 p.m., followed by quiet throughout the house till morning. The wooden lectern was replaced by the brass one and the flowers by a simple teak cross from India. For the earlier weeks of Lent we had been using

C

the book *Jesus Our Contemporary* by Geoffrey Ainger, a Methodist minister working in Notting Hill. We were challenged by his re-thinking of the Christian story in the light of the human need he met every day.

'On Thursday evening we celebrated the Lord's Supper, with the New Covenant and the foot-washing especially in mind. Friday morning prayers reminded us of the weary hours of the trial and death sentence. After two lecture sessions we went to the Three Hour Service at St John's Episcopal Church. People who have not previously been to such a Service are usually apprehensive and then amazed to find how fast the time goes.

'We came back to the usual Friday Open House; in the evening a large group went to hear Bach's St John Passion in the Usher Hall. Others went to Cephas and were impressed with the group of some 200 young people who congregate there, as well as those, often of the same age, who are there as "helpers", using every chance to get to know the club members and to be available when needed.

'At 11 o'clock on Saturday night nine of us went to the Holy Cross Roman Catholic Church to take part in the Easter Vigil. We had asked members of the Grail for advice and they kindly invited us back to breakfast afterwards.

'It was a most impressive service, in English, helpfully explained by the priest as he went through it. It began outside the church with the lighting of the Paschal candle and then, from that light, of the candles held by all. During the service there were three representative readings, the blessing of the baptismal water, an adult baptism, and renewal of baptismal vows by the congregation. Mass was celebrated, the Gelineau version of the Psalms being used, and we finished with Lauds at about 1.30 a.m. Then to the Grail residence for boiled eggs, rolls and tea, and home to bed about 2.30 on a clear moonlit night.

'Some of the students were up before 6 to go and fry sausages with a Youth Fellowship on the foreshore, others to take part in a 6 a.m. Communion Service at the Old Kirk, Pilton. Later everyone met on the College stairs for the Easter greeting before going singing into Chapel. The short service included a dramatic reading of the encounter of Mary with Jesus in the garden, some words of Emil Brunner, hymns and prayers. It ended with the singing of the Chinese hymn "Won the Victor's Crown" with percussion accompaniment. Thence to breakfast, with tables set in a horseshoe and Scandinavian candles for decoration.

On Sunday afternoon, after records of Easter music from the Russian Orthodox Church, a German Jazz Mass and Sidney Carter, some students met Junior Sunday school children to take Easter eggs to a school for small handicapped children. Thanksgiving Service with visitors from two Youth Fellowships brought to an end our Easter celebrations.'

A student of 1963 sums it up: 'There were many experiences at College—the intensity of studying; the effort of public speaking; the tiredness; the refreshment of the spring-like beauty of worship in Chapel; the family-of-Christ feeling; the togetherness and loneliness of community living; the broadening of the mind and the maturing of the spirit. The result was *God Confidence*. St Colm's did not mould me into a missionary confident in my own learning and knowledge. I learned that I was not able for everything. And so I emerged from St Colm's sadly shaken, on my knees, but with great joy—and God confident.'

The staff member responsible for Chapel was involved in constant commitments—drawing up the rota and lectionaries, overseeing the Chapel section in their Saturday cleaning, preparing for services, keeping books accessible and in order, preparing for special occasions and Communion services with the allotted group. She was also the person to whom people turned who were taking prayers for the first time, or who felt they knew nothing about the subject for intercession, or who wanted advice on where to find suitable help in the well-stocked devotional library and College files.

In the late sixties it was agreed that there should be a Chapel Committee. With an enthusiastic student group this came into being. The group met once or twice a term to decide upon forms of service, giving due consideration to suggestions before they were tried out in Chapel.

Now and again, late in the session when people knew each other, a group might be asked to prepare special prayers together; some of these services which were related to group Bible Study are included in the Church of Scotland publication *Clues*. This proved valuable for discovering that what one wanted did not necessarily appeal to another and that the leadership of corporate prayer is not in the least simple.

Drama

Drama, art, music, poetry and novels found their natural way into study and recreation. It was a great occasion for the College when eventually Edinburgh opened its Gallery of Modern Art in the Botanic Gardens across the road. One student, on entering what she feared might be an almost unbearably restricted College life, rejoiced at one of the first questions—'Are you interested in acting?'

Drama as a means of worship, of probing into meaning, of releasing latent talent has always featured in the College programme. Early records speak of dramatic readings by the fireside, of scenes from Shakespeare, the Golden Legend, Mahabharata, Jane Austen, George Eliot. In 1916 the dramatic presentation of *The Light of Asia*, a study in Buddhism by Sir Edwin Arnold, was given at a College gathering, expressing vividly the spirit and life of another continent.

Miss Small adapted her book *Yeshudas* to represent through drama and music the spiritual quest of India. Staff and students appeared in this Act of Worship at gatherings both far and near, expressing its message through narration and Indian song.

Discovery through drama continued in varied forms— meaning was clarified in parable, in Old and New Testament events, in the application of Christianity to current happenings. Drama often took the form of mime, especially in Advent, when a Narrator read from the Bible and the choir sang appropriate carols from the Oxford Book. Plays concerning the Christmas and Easter Festivals were learnt, rehearsed and produced within the College and performed in hospitals, churches and clubs. At other times a group wrestled with a study of the Bible event and there emerged their own interpretation and form of presentation.

At the women's meeting, where the Christmas Festival of Song and Drama took place from earliest days, the student group in war-time 1941 enacted a series of events in the life of ordinary people, using Old Testament words as translated by Dr Moffat—a woman who had known better days packing her case to go into a home for the destitute, a family in central Europe suffering oppression and famine, a German pastor under persecution, three women struggling to keep going: a business woman, a woman of the world, a scholar. Each scene pictured hopelessness and despair. There followed the Nativity scenes, the *New* Testament, the promise, expressed by solo and choral speaking, carols and anthems, the Good News that Christ met every need.

A moving performance was given in March 1941 of Tolstoy's *Michael*, in St Bernard's Hall. In 1942 a play was chosen which gave in modern speech an enjoyably realistic version of the Church at Corinth before Paul's letter arrived, followed by the effect of the letter—the actors greatly appreciating giving voice to the turgid controversy which ensued. These various plays were a significant means of involvement and worship, of reverence and inspiration.

During the fifties and sixties drama proved to be a particularly creative group activity in the programme of Christian Education. After one or two sessions in the Communication Class, the idea was introduced to the whole College that they might create their own Christmas play. Everyone discussed themes—The light shineth in the darkness, Release to the captives, The Hope of the world, God with us, What's the use of Christmas? It was surprising how little the students knew of the actual Christmas narrative. They came together to work out for themselves what they felt was the message of Christmas, to whom they wanted to present it, and what volunteers could be prevailed upon to write, produce, act, read, sing and stage-manage. The staff stood back in the guise of 'an enabler'. It was a gruelling but exhilarating operation. A small group then wrestled over the preparation of a script, using singing, reading of scripture, commentary and scenes acted or mimed: a setting in which the audience could join through well-known hymns.

It took many hours to hammer out the form of presentation, the group approach being especially valuable for ministers and teachers accustomed to individual preparation. Ideas such as portraying human sacrifice or converting Herod

were sadly rejected—'It's not in the Bible' seemed a feeble
argument.   More than one Presbyterian minister saw little
need for introducing Mary; 'I suppose you'll need someone
to hold the Baby' was the reluctant compromise.   Many
and strange misunderstandings of Scripture and human
nature came to light and much was learned through clash
of interpretation.

The medicals helped the producers to understand that
singing, colour and movement were especially helpful to
sick and elderly people; the prison staff set the background
for valuable understanding of the audience there.   Productions took place in hospitals—general, geriatric, mental;
in prisons, churches and fellowship groups.   'Release to
the Captives' was linked with World Refugee Year; 'The
Hope of the World' with prison, mental hospital and a
group of pensioners.

Miss Gray, accustomed to writing and producing plays
for some years, acted as general supervisor.   She writes:
'Eventually all was ready for casting, for brief rehearsals in
groups, and finally for departure to our captive audience.
After a simple, meaningful time of prayer in Chapel we
set off—students, boarders, teaching staff and household
staff.   Our carefully thought out presentation might possibly
have been over the heads of the men in prison, but the
Governor told us that what had meant most to some who
sat with tears streaming down their faces was the sight of
Joseph leading Mary the whole length of the prison chapel.
They were not to know that Joseph was a Dutch doctor
who had just welcomed his first baby to St Colm's, and
that Mary was a German teacher.   It's a long time, if ever,
since these men saw a man helping a woman with such
gentleness and love, was the explanation.

'One year we produced a significant Act of Worship with
no Mary, Joseph, shepherds or wise men, but as always

trying to show how relevant Christmas is to ourselves. Another year, when we had a small number of students, we used slides of famous paintings from many periods and countries—including modern Africa and India. In 1969 we produced a service for the Third Sunday in Advent using as our basic group Bible Study and relevant passages in the Lectionary of the Church of South India. We developed the themes of Promise and Judgment, the Coming of Christ, His work on earth, the call to His Church, illustrating our presentation by extracts from the World Council of Churches Uppsala Conference—Barbara Ward's speech and extracts from Dr Visser t'Hooft, and finding the relevance for ourselves today in the song *Magnificat Now* and a reading from Dr Martin Luther King's memorable sermon "I have a Dream".

'Our productions were never brilliant, but they were memorable to us who were united by our offering and to the audience who were caught up in our enthusiasm. Christmas was shared.'

Another Christmas Act of Worship is described by a Home Mission student: 'The Christmas Play was always something of a miracle. The writing was a group production, partly in verse, partly prose, the dialogue being talked into being and then written. One year the shepherds were the principal characters. They saw the light on the hills, were turned away from the busy inn, and at last found the baby and set off to tell the world. They erupted, crooks and all, into the living-room of a bad-tempered modern family to whom they proclaimed the God Here and Now. Then, because the players were going to a children's ward in a T.B. Hospital, there followed a scene of children being visited by St Nicholas. The modern family, the shepherds and the children all returned to the stable to lay their gifts at the feet of the Child.

For as we told our message on our way
we found that we could only say
one thing
A Child is born who shall be king
if you will crown him so.
And some there were who sneered and turned away
And some there were who said 'Yes, we will go
to meet the King.'
And here they come . . .

'Choir and players usually rehearsed in sections and rehearsals were often catastrophically bad. Everyone was busy, some were having injections. To quote from a party piece:

' ''Now after the cessation of the plagues, the saints found that the batteries of their torches were quite flat. . . . And about this time the saints began their struggle with the preparation of an Advent Play. A rehearsal was called and lo! the shepherds were smitten with stiffness, Adam's knees shook with bashfulness and cold. . . . And the clouds darkened over the house. . . . But the days passed and with the coming of Advent a baby arrived and two of the saints were betrothed and two other saints dedicated for their journeys. And the Advent Play was presented and it was good.''

'One of the great features of the play was the setting forth, after prayer in Chapel, of the whole College family bent on this missionary enterprise. Another feature was the arrival at the hospital and the setting up of lights and props with care so as not to inconvenience the ward. Then the audience assembled and the magic began. But without the search for understanding, the meticulous planning, the inspiring leadership, none of the Christmas plays of this period would ever have seen the light. Magic does not happen of its own accord. But there it was—only the

c*

music of the carols, only coloured lights, only costumed figures enacting a familiar story, but somehow mystery, enchantment, excitement and promise. Much more than a play: always a Happening, an Act of Worship.'

Communication through visual exhibits

The Student Day Annual Sale, held during the meeting of the General Assembly, was an opportunity for presenting to the public the aim and wide-flung interests of the College. To do this it was customary as a group activity to prepare an exhibit, stressing each year a different facet of College life and service. A number of students undertook to work out the theme and set up the exhibit in a large room where the process could be pictorially and symbolically represented, no mean task when it meant giving reality to such subjects as

> Jesus Christ, Light of the World
> The Changing Pattern of Mission
> What is the Church?
> The story of St Colm's College.

It is impossible to represent adequately this visual process in words; some idea may be conveyed by a short description of the 1964 Exhibit entitled *What is the Church?*

Based on the text 'He calleth his own by name and leadeth them out' (the theme of the Chapel window) and the key words Almighty, Laity, Dialogue as used in the year's mission study, the Exhibit showed what was implied by obedience to the call. The first wall in the room illustrated the Church as the People of God, called and commissioned, one poster depicting varied types of homes—rich and poor, in climates temperate and tropical—indicating that Jesus could come into the lives of all alike. One arm of a crossroads led to the model of a church, where members shut themselves into their own exclusive club named 'Dead

End'. Some were chained to their pew, some bowed down before their minister in his high pulpit, others harangued God with their monologues, blind to the purpose of dialogue; all refused to recognise the ordination of the laity. These were the Christians who refuse to obey the call.

Another road led to a poster showing the previous homes with a church in the centre. Some footsteps led from the home to the church and stayed there (once-a-week Christians); others led from home to church and back again (insurance Christians); others led from home to church to other homes (missionary). The next poster enlarged this last theme by showing those who witnessed—child and teacher in school, teenager in café, mother at the shop, father in the factory. The footsteps led on to another poster showing a globe made up of magazine pictures of very varied people—'And there shall be one fold, and one Shepherd.'

The second wall illustrated Preparation, 'That they might be with Him'—men and women—both in college and in the Church at large—growing in knowledge of the Bible, the Faith, Worship, the World, so as to witness within the congregation, in everyday life, in full-time service.

The last wall showed those about to leave the College, indicating the kind of work they would be doing. Alongside were pictures of people doing similar work in this country and overseas, all alike engaged in mission. The Exhibit finished with the words, 'Go ye . . . this is for all of us.'

Visual presentation of Bible truth, of theological terms, of man's need, or of an Act of Worship was an exacting means of expressing discovery through study; posters or other media wrought out of such searching could be used by students in their contact with Youth Fellowships and other groups—a challenging talking-point leading below the surface to understanding in depth.

CHAPTER SIX

The Bible—A Quest

STUDY of the purpose and content of the Old and New Testaments was always a vital part of the College curriculum. Knowledge was conveyed in various ways—by lecture, seminar, individual study, visual demonstration, group study, Sunday school preparation, drama, Chapel services.

Group Bible Study has since 1931 been an important feature of College life. It rose out of the early 'Conference' method as well as from the study of the Bible in the Sunday School Training class. Miss Harris and Miss Chell were concerned at the lack of biblical understanding shown by many students. Stimulated by the writings of T. R. Glover —*The Ancient World* and *The Jesus of History*—the class delved into the geographical and historical cross-references in the revised edition and studied the setting of the passage and the detailed text, preferably without commentaries. Students were helped to formulate questions and to prepare to lead the group study. The intention was to exercise research— both individually and in a group—not in order to find a tidy answer, a final irrevocable conclusion, but to give directive to the ever-present quest, to cut through facile platitudes based loosely on 'what the Bible says', and to realise afresh the contemporary relevance of the passage.

During the early forties the Eight Questions method formulated by Susanne de Dietrich demanded concentrated study; various modern translations were used in addition to the Revised Version. The method guided the group first to pause and listen to the actual text of the chosen passage, to discover the real question posed by the writer, his intention in recording the story, then to visualise the scene and the persons involved, and having thus examined the text to try to express its central meaning. The next step was to apply this meaning to the local church, to public affairs and personal life and to any practical act of obedience that might follow, and then to consider what directive it could have for life-in-relationship. A personal record of the study was afterwards written by each member of the group.

The questioning group came increasingly to realise the basic conviction expressed through the Bible—that of Purpose, and through their conflict of thought and opinion, their flashes of personal insight and group discovery they realised afresh signs of that purpose in the life of mankind—past, present and to come.

They learnt anew how to ask, seek, knock. Freed from the limitations of finality, they came to see life as perpetual quest and discovery within the context of purpose.

Bible Study became a confrontation with the living God mediated by biblical witnesses. To those unaccustomed to this expectant approach the Chapel sermons given by Miss Macnicol were a stimulating revelation. Students caught the desire to think for themselves and pierce through to the human element within the all-too-familiar text. A few extracts from these sermons are as good a means as any of illustrating the originality and gaiety that infected the weekly Bible Study. Miss Macnicol ruminates on Manna in Exodus and Numbers: 'Numbers is realistic and human in its picture—Israel's yearning for melons and cucumbers, and Moses' fed-upness with the burden of responsibility, and the quails making them all sick! Exodus is much more

priestly—the spiritual significance of the whole business and
its relation to spiritual food (the sabbath)—'Man doth not
live by bread alone.' It relates to *how* one gets one's
livelihood—how one approaches the business of earning
one's living—recognising it is from God and that therefore
it must be done in His way, not for personal greed or
excessive profit, but for the life of the whole; it does not
demand all one's time and energy—seven days' food for
six days' labour is the Exodus teaching.'

To students confused by the harsh encounter in College
of differing interpretations, the pain of misunderstanding
and the fear of challenge to traditional belief, one sermon
speaks, based on St John 4: 1-42.

'In His passage through the wilderness of this world the
Lord (who is Jesus) comes to a well. And to that well,
from the other direction, comes a woman. And so they
meet—at Jacob's well, the well of the ancient tradition of
Israel, used daily by this woman hundreds of years later.
It is what God does—speaks to us in our inheritance, the
things we have received from our families, our parents.
Then the familiar and stable background of our lives suddenly
becomes the place where God meets us.

'The meeting begins with a request from God—how
courteous he is in his dealings with us. He comes to meet
us but he never forces himself upon us. . . . Then there
comes the extraordinarily baffling conversation—two
people, each speaking a language of their own—a language
of heaven and a language of earth. See how the woman
picks up what Jesus says and immediately interprets it in
terms of her own limited outlook. She's a person who
knows quite a lot about Church history—about Jacob, about
the difference between Jews and Samaritans, about worship
at Jerusalem and at Mount Gerazim, about the Messiah—
but it is all somehow dead knowledge, a dark dank well

instead of living, rippling water; shut in, confined, instead of flowing freely hither and thither and watering all the places of life. She knew it all, particularly perhaps on its negative side—but it hadn't done much to help her own life, it did not seem to touch her home situation. Yet Jesus goes on, giving her those wonderful words of eternal life—never letting her know how silly she is, never giving her up as hopeless, pouring out for her the glory of heavenly truth even though she twists it into some queer meaning—her description of himself to her fellow townsmen.

'It is what God is always doing with us, not patronising us by giving us fairy-stories in place of truth, but giving us patiently the fullness of his truth, even when we mess it about so much. We cramp it inside our own limited experience, we try to shut it in instead of letting it flow freely. Much of it is probably beyond our reach and understanding, but *living*, not dead as it is when we try to grasp it and hold it still, trying to comprehend God instead of letting him hold us. No wonder God becomes weary in his dealings with us. And yet the struggle, the incomplete understanding, can never be abandoned by him—it is the meat he eats, the source of being and life to him. This is something to remember as we seek to speak the language of heaven to people who seem to understand so little and to misunderstand so much. This conflict is God's gift of life to us. We enter into an inheritance of unceasing labour and it is our *life*, as the work of the fields is the life of our bodies. It does not matter that their interpretation and ours differ—what does matter is that a life should be communicated.'

The Meaning of Christmas—Extracts

. . . 'What is the heart of it all? A new creation: Genesis 1 tells us of the meaning of our world, stage by stage, layer by layer, till it reaches the climax of human development, which is the final stage for the writers of the Old Testament—God rested thereafter from his creation. There is development after that but no new creation until that first Christmas when the Spirit of God which moved upon the waters at the beginning of creation moved again, and on earth appeared God's new creation, the man Christ Jesus—a man, but more than mere man, even as man is both animal (the previous stage in creation) and something more than animal.

'It is so easy to think of our world, our universe, as a closed system, able to develop new combinations of existing elements perhaps, full of unexplored possibilities and unknown quantities, but nevertheless closed. Creation has ended—that is, the making of something out of nothing (as we would say), out of the outer nothingness that surrounds our universe—that kind of thing has ceased. God once created, but in that respect he has been resting ever since, maintaining his handiwork, renewing it, bringing forth new developments, but not *creating*. Christmas checks us here; less than two thousand years ago, well within the limits of human history (let alone earth's history) we have a *new creation*. God is still Creator, ours is not a closed system, it is always open to the unknown which lies beyond.

'Those of you who knit know that there are two ways of joining in new thread—you tie a knot, the beginner's way, or you unravel the strands of the old thread, insert the new and twist it all together again so that the whole seems an unbroken thread, the way of a skilled knitter. God is no beginner, so you find no knots in the thread of his handiwork —the joins are not visible.

'In a sense this is like the new creation that God made when first he produced mammals in a world of reptiles, or human beings in a world of animals—in a sense, but not entirely because *outwardly* there is nothing new—in body Jesus is the same as any man. This new creation is entirely in the realm of the spiritual life and that means that we on this earth are ushered into a new world. It is not just God's activity that has been at work—God himself has entered our world and entering has brought us into the freedom of heaven. That is why those words are used of Christ, 'begotten not created', and at his birth the angels, the inhabitants of heaven, are visible to men.'

In a community as mixed as St Colm's—with ministers and lay people, graduates and non-graduates, Scots and overseas students, men and women—there arose the question as to whether all study should be graded and suited to the particular stage of each group. To a large extent this was, of course, done; timetables were tailored even to individual requirements. But activities common to all also have their value; worship is an obvious one. Perhaps not so obvious, but equally valuable, was the weekly Bible Study programme.

Here there was a quite deliberate 'stirring of the pot' in order that the groups into which students and staff divided should be a real cross-section of the community. For this was not an academic exercise but a practical inquiry into the Word of God for life, and for this all kinds of knowledge and experience—whether theological, pedagogical or practical—are equally valid. For young ministers straight from specialist studies in Old or New Testament it was not always easy to adjust to a situation in which their contribution as biblical scholars was not necessarily the major factor alongside the wise comments based on experience which nurses, teachers, builders or others had to offer.

Without doubt Group Bible Study was an experience of revelation for all who participated wholeheartedly, and especially valuable for ministers whose training tended to

equip them to speak and lead rather than to listen and share.
Members of staff acknowledge thankfully how much they
learned from these groups through united search for what
God had to say.

This challenge to pause—to examine pre-conceptions—
to allow for new interpretation—to sweat mentally—to
seek stillness emotionally—is a severe test and can be
shattering. The testimony of many throughout the years
is that this experience proved to be a costly but lasting
inspiration.

Study techniques varied and stimulating methods kept on
emerging. In the early sixties one result of experimenting
in groups was the publication by the Church of Scotland
Youth Committee of three study books with the title *Clues*.
One of these was a workbook on the Parables using the
results of a Group Bible Study at St Colm's.

Many methods were used. During the first hour,
following the students' own preparation, studied the text
using research, similar to the Eight Question method,
then groups undertook tasks giving an application of the
message of each parable in turn. This took the second
hour of a two-hour period and the first hour the following
week. During the last hour everyone came together and
shared the results of each group's discoveries and had
general discussion. One group found out what the parable
would mean to those who heard it for the first time and
for whom the evangelists recorded it in the Gospels.
The second group tried to put the parable in a modern
setting—much more difficult than might be imagined; the
third group prepared the outline of a talk, a sermon or a
Bible study for a specific group. The fourth group worked
out their response in worship, choosing or writing hymns
to suit the theme, with Bible readings and prayers. This
Act of Worship was carried through in Chapel by the group

at prayers next morning or evening. Drama, posters, blackboard illustration and models were used to illustrate the group findings, and everything was kept as topical as possible, for example illustrating points from things seen and heard at the General Assembly and using newspaper headlines.

A lively assertive exchange took place in a discussion on 'Take no anxious thought for the morrow'. In each group there was a role-playing Hedonist, Marxist, Hindu, Canaanite Pagan and harassed housewife—the Hedonist proved the most unruly; the passage sprang to life.

The study of Jesus and the Children led to consideration of what points would be appreciated by five to seven-and-a-half year olds, followed by preparation of the lesson for that age group. A difficult but effective course was held on the study of Words in the Bible following the New Mexico Study Outline, such key words as Create, Reveal, Reconciliation, New Creation, Covenant, etc. After searching study each group prepared some expression of their understanding of the word—an Act of Worship, a Sermon outline, a Bible Study plan for a definite age group. The following week all met together to present their efforts. In the study of the word Covenant they drew up a dialogue presenting man's type of covenant as compared with God's. All assignments were demanding, a few alarming—after the study on 'One God the Creator' suggestions were as follows: Agree on a definition of 'Create'—write in your own words what God the Creator means to you; write a modern Psalm on God the Creator; prepare a poster to illustrate convincing proofs of the power of God's spirit. Frequently there was the suggestion to illustrate the theme pictorially or to compose a psalm, hymn or dramatic presentation. All practical expression was based on study, discussion and team work.

Group Bible Study ranged over many parts of the Bible and always the individual was directed towards a probing for fact and meaning. The subsequent task ensured that there was immediate practical application of truth discerned. Following upon a study of the Acts of the Apostles groups were asked to sum up what the studies meant to them and how they could relate the result to their own lives, to the world and to the church of today—one wrote a Credo, one an Act of Worship, and one created in pictorial form the life and witness of the Church and man's response. Study of the labourers in the vineyard ranged from readings of the diary of the wife of one of the labourers to the latest dock strike.

The methods of the fifties and sixties illustrate other means of giving people a working knowledge of the Bible as a whole and some clues as to how to use it; weaning them away from dependence on commentaries (especially of one point of view) while helping them to use tools such as atlases, reference books, concordances, etc.

Miss Fraser introduced the course with one period of 'The Bible on the Blackboard'. This meant taking a broad theme, e.g. The Activity of God in the World, before and after Christ, the cosmic setting starting with pre-history: a garden, perfect relationship between God, man and nature, then stretching forward to post-history: Christ's kingly reign. Concentrating on revelation through Prophet, Priest and King, the tutor and the class work together to build up the sequence, the happenings, the persons, the outcome of this spiritual manifestation in the life of the People of God. In response to the suggestions from the class the pattern on the board begins to take shape, words become meaningful, the tempo quickens, and though the tutor has started with some conception of the evolving theme, nevertheless the exercise is organic, it is a group effort of lively participation.

This leads into a Course, continuously flexible and sensitive to events within the life of the College, a typical outline being as follows:

Talks on Biblical Interpretation.

1st Year: Survey of Old Testament, with reference to the Dead Sea Scrolls and Apocrypha. A synoptic Gospel, Paul's Epistles, St John's Gospel.

2nd Year: A study of Deuteronomy showing the People of Israel crossing frontiers and re-learning their faith in new situations. The Law travelled with them and grew to meet their changing circumstances—sound policy for the missionary.

A second synoptic Gospel.

Special studies such as healing, the place of women, the meaning of Judgment, Ethics, etc.

One major Epistle. Pastoral Epistles, relevant to pastoral work to come.

Hebrews and Revelation—reflecting the Jewish and Christian Week and Year, the Paschal Liturgy and the Emperor Cult as related to Germany under Hitler—subjects interpreted by the writings of D. T. Niles and Hans Lilje.

'Thinking with the Bible' was the third term conclusion to Bible Study, helping people to relate what they already knew to situations in which they would be likely to find themselves, e.g. travelling from Bombay to Madras in a railway compartment with an Indian student who says he has never before had the chance of a conversation with a Christian, or meeting the casual remark: 'I'm as good as the next man, but I don't go to Church'; or making an effective point in a letter to the local paper.

This practical application began with a 'recall' of the Bible on the blackboard. Then were chosen some topical comments such as were found in the newspaper or had arisen in actual conversations:

> Christian preoccupation with sin is morbid;
> the report of a sermon claiming that the Church of Scotland was very weak in its attitude to divorce;
> scare reports about immigrants and unemployment.

The group then tried to review the biblical evidence as a whole (not by single texts) which had a bearing on the issue in question. This was done by taking students' suggestions, putting them in some kind of grouping on the blackboard, then eliminating and organising. They worked over it to produce a version which was convincing to themselves as a kind of card reference. On the basis of the discussion they then tried to compose the appropriate letter or decide on a form of action, submitting the results to comment and criticism.

There was at times a somewhat homespun exegesis. The Foolish Virgins parable gave rise to a motor saga in *The Weekly Journal* of 'The Five Foolish Youths' who, assigned to organising an Approved School party 'went down to Tynepark, in number a husbandman and four bachelors, in one horseless chariot which duly sickened and died, for the spirit had gone out of it. And they came unto the dwelling of a wise man and cried out: "Give us of your oil." And he would not. And the bachelors said unto the husbandman, "What shall we do?" And he answering spake, "Let us now push on, even unto Levenhall; peradventure we shall find there a man of spirit." So they continued a sabbath day's journey to request a watchman for oil. But he said: "Peradventure there will not be enough for us and for you; go rather to them that sell."

And the moral—'If any man compel thee to push his car one mile, go with him twain.'

On another occasion a group having studied this same parable were acting out an Indian wedding which is closely parallel to the Palestinian. Into this dramatic maelstrom of activity came two Danish visitors who registered transparent disbelief when Miss Fraser whispered: 'We're in the middle of Bible Study.'

From a Nigerian pastor came a comment about sheep: 'I wonder at God's care of such a troublesome animal.'

An example of thoughtful adaptation of the 23rd Psalm came from Cameroon:

The Lord is my herdsman,
I shall lack nothing.
He leads me as North to South (in dry months)
In green forest and by fresh rivers.
He restores strength in me.
He safeguards me against lorries.
Though I travel and sleep in darkness
I have no fear,
For He is awake, His voice comforts me.
He gives me food in presence of elephants and buffaloes,
He anoints my body against tsetse flies.
Surely grace and mercy shall overshadow me always.
And I will follow and trust Him
    As long as I live.

CHAPTER SEVEN

The College in Mission—Christian Education

CHRISTIAN Education has been an important feature of the Church in Scotland throughout its history. The dream of John Knox and the Reformers—to have a school in every parish, the father also being responsible for teaching the faith in his own family—was never fully realised. Here and there ministers began to supplement the teaching given at home, and there were at least five Sunday schools in Scotland before the year 1780 when Robert Raikes started the first English Sunday school at Gloucester, his aim being to combine literacy with instruction in the Catechism, the Prayer Book and the Bible.

In Scotland, Forteviot had a Sunday school as early as 1730; Sunday School Societies were formed in Glasgow and Aberdeen in 1787. There are records of prodigious feats such as memorising the books of the Bible as well as the Shorter Catechism. Questions were raised concerning non-ordained persons being entrusted with the teaching of the Faith. By 1824 Thomas Chalmers had arranged for kitchen Sunday schools, graded according to age, to be held in his Glasgow parish for instruction in the Scriptures and the Catechism. It was not until later that new concepts of education concerned with understanding the child gradually came to influence the Sunday School programme in Scotland.

Early Developments in Sunday School Method

From the first days of both Deaconess House and the Missionary Training Institute, lectures were given on Sunday school method, and students involved in teaching. In 1898 Miss Kate Hammer was appointed to assist Miss Small.   As one of the early women students at Newnham College, Cambridge, she was a natural pioneer, and her six years on the staff of Redland High School for Girls at Bristol made her an experienced educationalist.   As a teacher she combined a mathematical precision with a wide cultural interest and knowledge of the Humanities.   She studied the current approach to the child through the emerging science of psychology, tempering it with her practical knowledge of child behaviour.

At the College she undertook teaching and practical work concerned with the Children's Church (Sunday school), Girls' Clubs, Women's Meetings and District Visiting. As far back as 1900 she was lecturing on new education methods and the principle of grading; her weekly preparation class was open to Sunday school teachers within the city of Edinburgh.

In 1907 Miss Hammer spent a weekend at the newly established Westhill Training Institute for Sunday School Workers, Birmingham, in order to observe the primary methods being taught by Mr George Hamilton Archibald, the Principal.   Her position on the staff of a Church-centred training college gave her strategic opportunity for influencing the development of the graded method in Sunday school work in Scotland.

The association of the College with St Bernard's United Free Church began with the move to Inverleith Terrace in 1909.   The minister, Dr George Steven, an enthusiastic and understanding friend of the young, was appointed Chairman of the College Committee.   For some years two

ladies of the Church had been running a flourishing Infant
Sunday school; a third member had attended a course at
Westhill and on her return had organised her morning Bible
Class into a group of Primary Sunday school teachers,
developing the Infant School into a Primary Sunday school.
Miss Hammer was subsequently asked to conduct the
Training Class for Teachers at St Bernard's and later became
responsible for superintending the Primary Department,
working with a combined team of members of the congregation and College students, an excellent project for the
College training programme.   The Department served as a
model for the new method, with its furnishings and
expression work suitable for young children.

Whereas in the early days of the Sunday school the
emphasis had been on Bible stories, the learning of psalms
and long scripture passages, coupled with a thorough
knowledge of the Catechism, the pioneers of the Graded
Sunday School saw the communication of the Word of God
and the life of Jesus as part of the total activity of worship,
the Service being as important as the lesson, and the whole
built up towards a related unity.

Miss Hammer's book, *The Sunday School of Today—the
Primary Department* did much to encourage the formation of
the Primary Leaders' Association which held its first meeting
in Edinburgh in 1915.   She was also alive to the importance
of hymns being related to the child's experience and
interests and later took a large part with Dr Herbert
Wiseman in the preparation of the Primary hymn book,
Children Praising.   Another valuable contribution was her
collaboration in the preparation of the new syllabus for
Primary and Beginners' departments, published by the
Scottish Sunday School Union.   This publication produced
for the under-fives a separate course and new presentation
of the story material, thus opening the way for the subsequent

development of the Beginners' Department, where the story was only one of the activities, the children taking part or not as they wished.

Additional experimentation in Sunday School development was provided from 1915 onwards through association with the Rev. George Stewart of Cairns Memorial Church. Miss Hammer and a team of students joined in visiting and teaching in his school of 350 children, where worship was real and reverent. In his booklet, *Worship in the Sunday School and Children's Service*, is expressed the oft-repeated principle, fundamental to the united worship of chidren with adults, that 'every act of worship must be treated as that which it professes to be'. This became the keynote in St Colm's training classes for all departments. 'It is useless to plan beautiful forms through which the children's worship may be offered if the children do not see in their worship and *ours* that every act is real.' This guiding principle directed the choice of hymns, the preparation of prayers and responses, the reading of the Bible and the offering of money. 'Reality is the source of reverence.'

Miss Hammer became widely recognised as an experienced authority in Christian Education and took an active part in Sunday School consultations planned by the Church. After thirty-three years of service at St Colm's she retired in 1931.

Miss May McKerrow, a member of Cairns Memorial Church and closely associated with the Reverend George Stewart in the promotion of Sunday school work, was one with whom Miss Hammer collaborated in the development of Christian education in Scotland.

In 1920 the Youth Committee of the Church, stimulated by the energetic determination of Miss May McKerrow, their Field Secretary, extended their resources and collaborated with the Missionary Training College in adding to the building and appointing a fourth member of staff to be responsible for training in Sunday school and youth work as an integral element in the College curriculum. This extension, coupled with Moubray House, provided accommodation for thirty-six students.

The Graded Sunday School

Miss Beryl Harris was appointed in 1931 to succeed Miss Hammer. She held the Diploma of the National Froebel Institute, London, also the Religious Knowledge Certificate of the University of London, and she had attended a course at Westhill College, Birmingham in Christian Education and Youth Work. She had had several years of teaching experience and was alert to changing patterns.

Miss Catherine B. Chell, B.A., served on the staff from 1930–1937 and worked closely with Miss Harris in Sunday school development. She came from the English Congregational Church and had had varied assignments in junior and adolescent work in Manchester, specialising in drama. At College she took the regular classes in Old Testament studies and principles and practice of Youth Work, while supervising the College Ranger Company. At Charteris Church she coped successfully with a demanding youth programme of Junior Club, Guides and Brownies. To the Sunday school she brought new insight and stimulating methods.

Graded Sunday school work had by the early thirties become well established and the need for planning fully recognised. In 1933 Dr Basil Yeaxlee, Principal of Westhill College, visited College for a few days and gave lectures and demonstrations on principles and method, as well as conducting an evening seminar in the common room to which interested teachers and ministers were invited. There were signs, however, that the teachers' grasp of the Bible was increasingly inadequate, and the College Training Class, introduced by Miss Harris and Miss Chell, became the pattern for the weekly preparation in each department of the Sunday school.

A new experience for teacher and child was the method used in the Beginners' Section for under-fives. Understanding came through doing, secular and religious life were one whole. The student came to see how the themes of Creation, Incarnation, Redemption could be presented through play activity, visual aids, informal drama and story. Only through her sensitivity to spiritual values, her own faith and practice, could the teacher enter wholeheartedly into this way of worship, finding with the children inspiration and delight in the Lord.

To the participating student this approach was sometimes a complete reversal of her conception of teaching. Accustomed as she was to verbal communication, she discovered that the story, though important, was the tiniest part of a varied and flexible Service, preceded as it was by looking at pictures round the walls and acting out situations to give content to the words and ideas in the story. 'We went shopping, we made scones for tea, we set the table so that tea would be ready for the big boys and girls coming home from school. We sank exhausted to the floor and discovered that Mummy did so much for us because she loves us and wants us to be strong and happy. We had experienced a little of the cost and joy of love, no moral had to be added. Singing, activities, prayers were spontaneous, children joined as they were able, yet there was a clear theme running through the whole programme.' Another student found unaccustomed freedom through this approach—'How do children learn to use words? Not by teaching them to say the sound, but by the "click" which takes place when a word like *hot* relates to the experience of heat—your foot in the bath water, touching the stove, burning your tongue. We relate words to experience. In religious education we teach mere sounds far too often—redemption, salvation, forgiveness, useless unless linked to experience.

'My thinking and teaching has been deeply influenced by this approach through experience; it was basic to Beginners' Sunday School in which St Colm's was far ahead. Later when I came to work with youth clubs inside or outside the Church, or to run camps for teenagers little connected with the Church, it was this principle that guided me.'

A university graduate from Northern Ireland, who also held a diploma in education, found the St Colm's training indispensable for her work as a Sunday School organiser. Twenty years after leaving College she recalls her enriching experience in the weekly training class:

'It is Lent. The subject for Sunday is some aspect of God's creative work evidenced particularly at spring time. We begin, not with the Bible or teachers' magazine, but with a bowl of scilla bulbs being placed carefully on the table—the flower is in bloom, there has been growth. "Lent" comes from an old word "lenten" which means "to grow". God is the source of all life and growth. How are the children in your class being helped to grow?

'By the end of the training class I had not only been helped in the preparation of the story, the worship, teaching aids and activities for the coming Sunday, but I had had an experience of renewal, of new insight. This "experiential" approach considered today to be new was the approach opened up for me two decades ago at St Colm's.'

The Family Church

The close association between family and Church had long been fostered by *the Cradle Roll*. A secretary within the Sunday School kept the list of babies baptised in the

Church up to date and visited the homes.   Three times a year mothers were invited to bring their babies to attend a service in the Primary Department; fathers sometimes came as well.   The children gave posies of flowers to the mother for the baby, and in the spontaneous atmosphere of the Primary Department there was a togetherness in the Lord between parents, children and teachers.

At the St Bernard's Davidson Beginners' Department, the fact that mothers took their share in teaching demonstrated the value of closer union between home and Sunday School. This resulted in increased attendance at the Young Mothers' Group in the Church Hall, mainly concerned with the question of upbringing.   House meetings were welcomed as bringing together a smaller, intimate group.

This concern for family life led, under the direction of Miss Harris, to the formation at St Bernard's Davidson of the Family Church in the autumn of 1944.   The term suggests its purpose, requiring the consent and active co-operation of the congregation, the emphasis being to bind Church and Sunday School into one fellowship.

A sponsors' secretary was appointed, members of the congregation agreeing to have children, whose parents did not attend morning service, to sit in their pew for the opening twenty minutes.   At both Christmas and Easter, instead of the usual Sunday School session, all joined in family worship in Church, but it was not until Whitsun that the way was open for the first Family Church Festival at the morning service.   The worship was conducted by the Minister, the service was built up by contributions from the work of each department; this was a service long to be remembered.   In this scheme the programmes of the different departments were planned so that there was simultaneous experience throughout of the same aspect of the Christian Year.

This venture was started after a visit to St Colm's in 1943 by the Reverend H. A. Hamilton, Principal of Westhill and initiator of the Family Church scheme. Certain results emerged. Within the Sunday school the units were drawn together; the gulf between Sunday School and Church was bridged; boys and girls came to feel at home in the church and the congregation became aware of the child life in its midst. Visiting was filled with meaning as the Family Church gathered more parents into membership.

The experiment in St Bernard's Davidson came to an end after a few years in response to a request from the Youth Department that the Scottish Sunday School scheme be used throughout. Some modern Sunday School Schemes have incorporated one of the main ideas of the Family Church, namely a common theme running through every section, culminating in an act of worship in which every department participates as well as the congregation.

Staff Participation in Christian Education

During this period of expansion in Sunday School work the College maintained close links with the Church of Scotland Youth Department through its Director, Dr W. Wightman, and Sunday School organisers. Candidates were sent to the College for training as Youth Organisers.

After 1929, with the uniting of the training work of Deaconess House and the Women's Missionary College, some of the work which had been done at Charteris Memorial Church by Deaconesses was now undertaken by students at the Missionary College. It included Senior and Junior Sunday School, a Boys' and a Girls' Club, Women's Meeting as well as visitations in the area.

Later, as the Church of Scotland Religious Education programme developed at Simpson House under the scheme for Youth Leadership Training, Miss Harris became a regular instructor in courses for leaders. Her booklet, *With the Beginners*, one of a Sunday School series published by the Youth Committee, was widely used.

From the beginnings of the Practical Work programme in the College, each member of staff was responsible with a team of students for carrying out a particular project in Sunday School, Women's Meetings, Youth Clubs, Parish Visitation, and other such activities. On every possible occasion local leadership in congregation or club was encouraged and independence fostered. This staff involvement was valuable because it gave opportunity for demonstration of principles being taught; it ensured a realistic approach to both preparation and evaluation. It was a salutary check on the detached academic approach, and fostered understanding, sympathy and confidence between staff and students.

Miss Beth Davey, B.A., appointed to the staff in 1940, came from the Irish Presbyterian Church and was well qualified in Sunday School and Club work. At Charteris she was responsible for the transformation of the Junior and Senior Sunday School Departments into a Junior Church with its Church Council responsible for certain practical details and for planning and conducting special services. Boys and girls met together during the week to make equipment—collection bags, Bible covers and such essentials. On Student Day at St Colm's they manned their own Junior Church Exhibit, explaining it to visitors.

Children at that time were maturing earlier than formerly and all youth work was affected by this sophistication and lack of concentration. They were more interested in discussion than in listening to a teacher; their questions were not always easily dealt with. These teenagers were a lively challenge to the student team, new patterns emerged and the theological basis of teaching was explored

D

in depth. The curriculum at the Junior Church followed the graded scheme prepared for the Church of Scotland; the weekly preparation class at College gave opportunity for any necessary adaptation and students were encouraged to use their own insight in presenting the lesson.

The link between the Sunday School and the weekly club activities was a practical means of holding the group together.

Varied Scope in Practice Teaching

By the early fifties the changing pattern in St Bernard's Davidson and the union of Charteris Memorial and Pleasance churches, coupled with the need for a wider experience in Christian Education on the part of the students, brought about a loosening of ties. Teacher members of the congregations who had benefited from their years of participation took responsibility for Sunday School leadership.

Students were attached for their practical work to a variety of Christian Education efforts in Edinburgh churches. Instead of Sunday School work being concentrated on two parishes and organised from St Colm's through its training class, students were allotted to different departments in a variety of churches for a term, and attended training classes under local leaders, thus widening their experience of varying approaches.

Miss Effie R. Gray was appointed to the staff of St Colm's in 1955, after experience as Church Sister, followed by ten years as organiser for Sunday School and Bible Class with the Church's Youth Department. She re-introduced the placement of students in one department of a Sunday School or Bible Class for a definite period. This took place in a number of churches. She herself, with a revolving team of five to eight students, joined with the Junior Sunday

School teachers at St Stephen's Parish Church. Here the students were able to teach and to share in the leading of worship and in the organisation of the Department and its weekly Preparation Class.

Many of the children attending Sunday School had no other connection with the Church and found it a strange world with an unfamiliar language and set of values, thus providing excellent experience for mission candidates. One exasperated eight-year-old interrupted an Easter Service: 'You don't mean to say you believe in all this bosh about Jesus no' being dead?'

Expression work and activities of all sorts were encouraged: the children wrote their own hymns and prayers, dramatised the story and topics for thanksgiving, made books and models, and through links with students coming from and going to countries overseas, the children developed a wonderful sense of the world church. They loved their occasional visits to St Colm's.

Bible Class work with adolescents was not so easy to find as most ministers like to conduct this age group themselves. During the war years some students had helped in a large Bible Class in a new housing area. Group activities were possible and Bible Study brought forth lively discussion and drama. The St Colm's involvement with the Bible Class age group continued when Miss Mary Lusk joined the staff in 1957. She undertook responsibility for the Bible Class in St Bernard's Davidson Church in which a small number of students was able to help. The outcome of one of their programmes was published in the Bible Class leaders' textbook *Royal Mail*. The fourteen- to seventeen-year-old group studied *Letters to Young Churches*, paperback copies being available. They discovered that answers to their questions about life today could readily be found in those letters of old.

Students in their second year were now attached for practical experience to a certain parish where they took part on Sundays and one half weekday in church activities and deliberations. Preparation classes for such work were held either in College or at the church. Creative, experimental work was continuous. One student helped in the working out of a part of a Bible Class Kit being prepared for the Youth Committee and another tried it out the following year. Others took part in Bible Classes where they were working on a new programme of Christian Education.

Youth Fellowships for the late teenagers provided further valuable experience. Second Years attended these in their own congregations; students from overseas likely to be involved with young adults visited many types of Youth Fellowships and shared in the activities. Members were encouraged to visit St Colm's and sometimes attend the occasional Valedictory Service in Chapel. Students have gone as delegates to the annual Christian Youth Assembly of Scotland and have learnt much about what young people are thinking.

Experience in group work included the occasional planning and conducting of Day School Assembly Services by invitation of the school Chaplain. At one school for some fifty physically and sometimes mentally handicapped children St Colm's students were responsible, with their Tutor, for conducting School Assembly once a month and teaching in classes. They shared experiences with the children through pictures, action songs, singing and informal talks by those from overseas about their country and customs. The well-planned summer party in the College garden took the form on one occasion of a Fair, complete with stall on the tennis court, a ghost train in the basement, and an excellent puppet show.

Summer Church Schools

There had been many experiments with informal education during the summer months and in 1957 the Reverend Hugh C. Hamilton came to Edinburgh from the Southern States of America bringing well-tried teaching aids with a view to introducing Summer Vacation Schools to Scotland. Miss Gray shared in the first experiment at Craigsbank Church and thereafter for several years led Junior or Senior Groups in Lockhart Memorial Church. She and a group of students worked out the scheme and carried through the programme by which children, whether church attenders or not, are gathered informally for a week or two to discover for themselves new understanding of the Bible, the Church and the purpose of their lives. Help came from parents, Day School teachers and others interested; time allowed for discoveries to be made in new methods and projects, and these schools have spread through parts of Scotland and Ireland, St Colm's students being still involved as part of their vacation work.

Christian education in one form or another was an integral part of any youth activity undertaken by the students, whether Sunday School, uniformed organisation, programmed club or unstructured group. Realising how essential was the theological and psychological understanding of the individual as a whole person, they studied young people in their environment, their relationships, their reactions to people and events.

During the past ten years throughout the Christian world there has been emerging yet another revolution in Christian Education. The Church of Scotland has set up a Committee to examine the whole educational policy of the Church for all age groups. A Baird Research Scholar has been appointed and new schemes have been produced. St Colm's has been kept in touch with these developments and students have been examining the underlying principles and applying them where appropriate in their practical work. The need for thorough training and preparation is apparent if leaders and teachers are to understand and use to the full the opportunities afforded by the new schemes.

CHAPTER EIGHT

The College in Mission—
Practical Involvement

FROM the opening of the first home of the Institute at 31 George Square, the Principal sought contact with neighbouring churches and welfare agencies and established the vital link between the candidates and the needs of the community. Miss Small says of this essential aspect of the curriculum: 'It was, of course, impossible to introduce Foreign Mission students to their practical work; the best that we could do was to find for them sufficient contact with human life—with life as the great body of humanity must live it, life poor, hardened, toilsome, with narrow outlook.' The aim of the Study section of the College programme was seen by Miss Small as 'aiming at such knowledge and understanding only as shall set imagination, thought, motive, action, upon right lines.' The College continued to face continually the needs of students in relation to the demands of the service for which they were preparing. Practical work was no hypothetical exercise promoted in a void: it was the response of the Institute to the invaluable opportunity to serve in church and society, to learn through direct experience how they might best be linked with the far-reaching programme of Home Mission in Scotland.

Practical Activities

The early years of exploration gave rise to varied experiments. In the courtyards at the back of the allotted district were held open-air meetings addressed by the students in turn; the gatherings were large and attentive and proved a good recruiting ground for regular group work. *The Guild of Friendship*, for women from congregation and district, developed from the kitchen meeting with its ½d cup of tea, its devotional address and occasional social, and in time two women's groups became the responsibility of the College team, one in Henderson Row, one in Fettes Row. Students in turn, under supervision, spoke at the weekly meeting, expressing their own convictions, often with stumbling words but with sincerity. The Christmas Festivals were well planned, joyful occasions of worship through song and drama as well as items by the Junior Girls' Club; plays included dramatic scenes and songs from the market-place in Palestine, Tolstoy's 'Where Love is, God is', and for Easter, 'The Passing of St Bede', John Masefield's 'Good Friday' and Laurence Housman's 'Little Plays of St Francis'. Later productions are described in the chapter on Drama.

A Junior Girls' Club, later called the Rowan Club, had a lively programme including handwork, singing, dancing, drama, outings and well-planned projects based on study and expression work. The girls contributed to the Guild of Friendship Festivals through drama, song and dance.

The College has always sought contact with the educational and philanthropic agencies of the city. In 1908 it had already taken part in the Scottish National Exhibition where at the employees' pavilion a recreation centre had been set up for women and girls; three students went twice a week to serve in the canteen. Two students did special area visits in connection with the Health Department; later this developed into the Healthy Babies Project, a scheme by which babies were visited fortnightly. Others took turns in a monthly visit to the Magdalene Asylum—an approved school for girls—where they gave entertainment through music, games and readings and tried to get to know the girls.

In connection with all this work there was in College a weekly evaluation class with the Tutor, when previously appointed student 'critics' commented on programme, technique and relationship within the group under survey, a valuable exercise in judgment.

The move to Inverleith Terrace in 1909 gave excellent opportunity for official connection under Session auspices with the work of the St Bernard's South Mission district. The minister, Dr George Steven, gave every encouragement to the work entailed, being himself an educationalist as well as convener of the College Education Committee. He was well aware of the importance of first-hand contact with family and community in the training of those committed to serve in the Church at home and abroad. It was through Miss Alice Wyld, member of staff from 1910–1916, that this social service programme developed in accordance with the policy of fellowship and courtesy defined by Miss Small. Miss Wyld had attended classes run by the Edinburgh Association for the University Education of Women; she was well experienced in social work and was particularly interested in the development of the Church Sister movement. The plan of work in the South Mission area was based on an initial visitation by the students in many homes, 650 visits being paid in two weeks. A definite area was then allotted to the College.

Home Visiting and Observation Visits

Regular visiting in the district was an important part of student training; classes were held on the aim and method

D*

of visiting; there was full discussion of questions arising from the visits; contacts with home and family opened the eyes of the College group to unsuspected problems and to the fortitude of those faced by privation and unemployment. A Conference was organised by the tutor, Miss Elizabeth Craig, in 1923 on the difficulties and opportunities of visiting; it was attended by representatives of other student groups, the medical profession and a few foreign students, and was addressed by those concerned with Infant Welfare and Public Health.

Observation visits linked to classroom teaching and practical endeavour in clubs and kindergarten gave students a detached view of principles in action. A weekly discussion was then held on method, based on the students' observation notes. A number of those attending the Institute were destined for education work overseas; during the second decade of this century there was considerable concentration on methods in Education. Visits therefore included Day Nurseries, the Montessori class in Gillespie's School, the Tynecastle Supplementary School (Junior Secondary), St George's School (one of the early fee-paying schools for girls), Board Schools (Education Authority). They also went to typical free kindergartens, as well as various charitable organisations and the Women's Hospital, and one student at a time attended the weekly meeting of the Charity Organisation Society. As social work commitments grew, the range of observation was extended to institutions for the poor, the blind, the deaf and dumb, as well as the police Courts and the National Vigilance Association.

Play Centres

Miss Hammer pioneered in the development of the weekday Play Centre after its introduction to Edinburgh by Dr Harry Miller of the Pleasance Church, following its inauguration in London by Mrs Humphrey Ward.   In 1908 the first Play Centre was opened in St Bernard's Public School for two afternoons a week under volunteer auspices. Miss Hammer was asked to help in its development.   The Centre provided for thirty to forty children of three to nine years.   There was a programme of physical recreation, handwork, and imaginative expression through the dramatisation of fascinating stories of other countries—Russia, Japan, America, etc., which were illustrated by lantern slides and made real by the various nationals amongst the College students.   Activity was often based on a theme, such as the life of the Red Indians, and expression work was both enjoyable and creative.

After the College moved to Inverleith Terrace in 1909 another Play Centre was started at St Bernard's United Free Church under the supervision of Miss Hammer and with the assistance of the students.   This Centre was open to both district and parish and numbers varied from 50 to 80.   The programme started with action songs in the main hall, after which children of different age groups went into separate rooms for a variety of appropriate activities.   When the College team was depleted in the 1914 war years, two students came from the Edinburgh College of Domestic Science to give help, to gain from the experience, and to attend the College lectures given by Miss Hammer on Play Centre History and Method.   In the summer term, 1915, the College took partial responsibility for Play Centres arranged for children dispossessed of morning school through military necessity.   A 'free kindergarten' was opened in a local front room in the district; there was access to a small garden at the back.

Miss Harris undertook supervision of the Church Play Centre when she succeeded Miss Hammer in 1931.   During the second world war the Centre went far to relieve the anxiety of parents who realised only too clearly the unsatisfied needs of their young; volunteers came to help the depleted student group and attended the weekly preparation class where programmes were carefully planned, new singing games learnt and material prepared. Many students have testified to the value of such planning for keeping a large group of lively youngsters happily occupied.

Meeting as it did after school hours on account of the black-out the Centre was closed towards the end of the war. Subsequently for the pre-school child the Department of Health set up Day Nurseries as well as morning Play Centres. A number of Toddlers' Play Centres were established and run by the Women's Home Mission Committee of the Church of Scotland in Edinburgh, Glasgow and Aberdeen.

An appropriate sequence is that the Church now supports the recent increase in Play Groups for pre-school activity, run under the auspices of the Social Work Department with the help of many churches. A number of deaconesses take part in running these Groups, the Church of Scotland has appointed two deaconesses as full-time organisers; in collaboration with the Local Social Work Department and the Play Groups Pre-School Association they help to run training courses for Play Group leaders.

Summer camps to provide much needed holidays for members of the Women's Club are mentioned from 1922 and were initiated by Miss Elizabeth Craig. One year a house was taken for a month, during which time it catered for mothers with children, young people and Sunday School teachers while students did the chores. Holiday camps were held in the thirties in Rosewell Church Hall and students took part in camps run at Dundonald and Port Seton and at the Children's Holiday Home at Humbie.

Vacation assignments included work among the fisher-girls in Shetland and the Orkney Islands, and in the home for Mothers and Infants at Leith. Thus summer and Easter vacation experience expanded with the years; reports were shared and evaluation made at the beginning of the subsequent term.

The College building and grounds made hospitality possible. The croquet lawn and tennis court were made available to Club girls, two Y.W.C.A. Clubs, young Sunday School teachers, and once a week to business girls working in Princes Street. Groups connected with the practical work enjoyed annual outings in the lovely grounds.

Settlement House Experience

In 1918 an effective extension to the Social Study programme of the College was the acquisition of Moubray House, a beautiful sixteenth century building at 53 High Street. The purpose of this gift from Mr William Walker was to provide the College with a Settlement House for specialised practical work in a suitable area. Groups of two or three students took it in turns to go into residence at Moubray House for some six weeks and under the super-vision of the Warden they found excellent opportunity to share in the work of the neighbouring churches and welfare agencies and to specialise in dispensary and other medical work, in infant welfare and in district visiting. The life of this small community provided useful experience in problems of adjustment similar to those on the mission field. The House was also used as temporary accommoda-tion for Women Home Mission probation candidates and for refresher courses for former students on furlough. The 1939 war brought a decrease in student numbers, thus necessitating the relinquishment by the College of the Settlement.

Work among Women

It was in 1918 also that a far-sighted project stressing encouragement in democratic leadership was started in Cumberland Street. It was initiated by Miss Currie, Tutor on the staff of St Colm's, in the shape of a Working Women's Club, similar to the Toc H Women's Settlement in London, and housed after much search in a shop-cum-kitchen situated in an area where people tended to be aloof and consequently cautious at first about visiting the Club.

The practical programme of child welfare, health lectures, concern about juvenile employment, and cooking and dressmaking classes suited to a post-war shortage of materials gradually drew in the hard-pressed housewives. They elected their own committee and in collaboration with the class instructors ran a successful centre. Contacts were strengthened in the district; work was started among junior girls. Students from the College were involved in various activities, including class instruction, discussion groups, talks on other countries, current events and duties of citizenship. In the post-war election campaign the general and ward election meetings added zest to the programme.

The Club ran on democratic lines, the members themselves being responsible for deciding what activities to include; they conducted the meeting and provided tea themselves on any special occasion. Babies were relegated to a small nursery on the premises under the care of a volunteer, leaving the mothers free to engage in their own pursuits. The independent spirit of the group was a healthy warning against benevolent manipulation from outside.

The Guild of Friendship continued happily from year to year, filling different needs as they arose. The students of Miss Moinet's era will never cease to be grateful to her for the help and insight she gave in relation to meeting people, visiting, and joining in the Guild of Friendship in St

Bernard's Davidson Church. It was the time of the Depression when there was much unemployment and real need; the solid stone houses had been subdivided so that whole families lived in one room with very inadequate washing and toilet facilities. More than one student remembers taking a deep breath before plunging up two storeys of wooden stairs, hoping the door would open before she had to take another breath with its full impact of wet rotting wood and bad plumbing.

For these tenants, struggling for decency in bad conditions, a Jumble Sale was held each year through the Guild of Friendship. It was a triumph of organisation and insight. Clothing was obtained from friends; one student remembers announcing with glee to a startled Reports Class: 'Mrs Belcher asks Miss Moinet to keep one or two of her chemises for her.'

Miss Moinet impressed upon all the importance of respecting the dignity and independence of everyone. Nothing at the sale was to be given away; a small charge was made and the money given to help someone less well-off.

Tables were put up in the hall and the clothes laid out. Students had taken it for granted that it would be wise to wear old clothes; Miss Moinet looked at them quizzically. 'Do you not enjoy shop girls who are smartly dressed? You are the equivalent for these women—put on your prettiest blouses.'

The door was opened, the sale began. There was no rush and tumble, no 'first in gets all', none of the greed, envy and disappointment that so often goes with sales. It was all meticulously arranged—the first few to arrive were invited to look round and choose only one article from each stall. After a short period a bell rang and they could then make a further purchase. The next group were then admitted, and so it went on, a delightful social event to be looked forward to for months.

Miss Mackenzie defined the distinction between Social Service and Home Mission: 'Preparation for Home Mission work is bound to take into account the social conditions and problems which affect the lives of so many people in our land. We tried to give our students the background of social study which their service would require, but at the same time we realised that the central concern for Home Mission is evangelisation and the building up of faith. To this effect we used the twofold approach of visiting in the homes and the opportunity for fellowship and teaching provided by the Guilds of Friendship, the combined festivals at Christmas and Easter being occasions of special opportunity.' Staff and students learnt much from Guild members—courage in difficult circumstances, practical sympathy naturally expressed to those in need, faith which stood testing in sore trial, warm interest in college affairs, and outgoing hospitality at the members' annual party given for the whole Guild. Friendship was the operative word.

Youth Work—Clubs and Uniformed Organisations

Concern for youth work grew during the years and the demand for help with teenagers came more insistently from overseas. The Social Study programme was expanded and emphasis placed on development of leadership capacity within the group. A new Senior Girls' Club proved valuable in this respect; a committee of five club members took responsibility for planning the programme and conducting club meetings.

It was decided in 1919 to include experience with uniformed organisations. At the request of the College, the Boy Scout and Girl Guide Movements sent training officers into the College to conduct sessions. A Girl Guide Company, and later a Ranger Company, were formed within the College so that principles and method were learnt through practical involvement. In the Junior Sunday School, students helped with the formation of a Wolf Pack and a Brownie Company, and for older girls, a Girl Guide Company. By 1938 it was agreed in consultation with the County Commissioner that instead of running a College Ranger Company the students should join in training classes for Edinburgh Guide and Brownie work, and that the Course should be held for all at St Colm's in May and June. Subsequently some students continued to attend such training courses and were involved in Guide Companies, Brownie groups and Cub work. In more recent years the Chief Training Officer has regularly visited the College to conduct sessions on International Guiding and training methods. On more than one occasion the Scout trainers have helped with campcraft demonstrations; students have to a lesser extent shared in the work of the Boy Scout movement.

The Girls' Guildry, now called the Girls' Brigade, is run under the auspices of the Church in many different countries. While at College many students attending Guildry training courses and helping in Companies have found much that could be used for youth work at home and overseas. Two students were sent from Jamaica at different times before undertaking Girls' Brigade work in that island, and an Irish teacher, who watched her luggage sail to India while she waited for the visa that never came, subsequently became the G.B. Organiser in Jamaica. Several men students have served in the Boys' Brigade and have availed themselves of generous invitations to share in the training courses and to help with Brigades. The Life Boys, now the Junior Boys' Brigade, gave delight and despair to many women students. The visit to the College of one Leith Company with their Leaders has for some years been a highlight of the summer course on uniformed organisations, the boys being much impressed by the library and Chapel—'Caps off, boys,' hoarsely muttered one nine-year-old.

Facilities and areas for practical training varied over the years. In time isolated forms of youth work such as the Rowan Girls' Club were succeeded by an integrated programme by which energies were channelled into one or two centres where contact through Sunday School and Club took place at least bi-weekly. At Charteris Memorial Church, junior clubs for girls and for boys gave brisk opportunity for exploration into the validity of classroom theory.

Students continued to identify themselves with the concern of the Church over 'Youth and Religion'. Representatives from St Colm's attended a conference under that heading in Aberdeen in 1941 and learnt of the stern judgement passed by youth on the Church—static, afraid to denunciate wrong, content with the second best, lacking Christian witness, archaic in language and custom. This challenge awakened in the College a fresh realisation of their task in the service of the Church—to preach Christ crucified and risen, to speak out against evil, to give to youth their due responsibility in the worship and work of the Church, to seek together inward renewal.

Realising the lack of opportunity for adequate training of leaders with a sympathetic understanding of school leavers in a war-absorbed environment, the College obtained recognition as a Training Centre from the National Council of Girls' Clubs, thus enabling them to hold courses for the Certificate in Club Leadership.

Summer Camps

In connection with the Charteris youth work, one of the most exacting and rewarding experiences was the summer camps programme for girls and occasionally Life Boys.

These provided excellent initial training in the planning of accommodation, equipment, catering and budgeting, and in learning at camp how to cope with discipline and freedom and plan the daily programme together with campers. 'It was a series of adventures all the way through—adventures in living and working together, in resourcefulness in many different situations, and most of all in friendship with the boys and girls. Being real city children, they found certain aspects of country life which did not appeal, and even the toughest boys kept their distance from cows, while insect life was unpopular with boys and girls alike. There was real delight in birds and flowers and their log-books reveal the satisfaction they found in playing in the burns. The day began with morning prayers and ended with a camp fire and story and evening prayers. The last evening was planned by the campers; they gave thanks: 'We thank Thee for bringing us safely here, and for all the things we have seen, felt, heard, smelt and tasted. We thank Thee for the kids, fox, calves, cows, sheep, birds, flowers and butterflies. We ask Thee to take us safely home. Help us to be kind and helpful to those at home, especially to those who need us, not to be greedy, and make us share our things with others." '

This experience in the mid-forties gave students some understanding of the gulf for boys and girls between what they learn and experience in Sunday School and how they live during the week, how materialistic, secular and self-centred home and family life could be. Camp gave exceptional opportunity for contact with parents; mothers came to Charteris to talk about the children's holiday, to see photographs and to exchange information as to the children's reports, in some cases to tell of the effect within the home. This led to further meetings with parents when students explained the purpose of the weekly club activities

—handyman, church decorators, toys for tiny tots, European news service, drama, games and songs. The presence of students from Denmark, Germany, Jamaica, Sweden and Switzerland after the close of war had helped to awaken in the boys and girls a first-hand interest in post-war Europe, resulting in practical concern for reconstruction through compiling a weekly news-sheet, selling hand-made articles, and making Bible picture books for distribution through a Church of Scotland Hut in Germany.

Expansion in Field Experience

Lectures in the basic principles of social administration were well illustrated by an expanded programme of observation visits to hospitals, child welfare clinics and centres, special schools, nursery schools, approved schools, Schools for Mentally and Physically Handicapped, as well as to the Council Chambers, the Employment Exchange, Juvenile Courts and Voluntary Service Agencies.

By the mid-fifties the changing pattern in St Bernard's Davidson and Charteris Memorial Churches set free more time in the practical work programme for observation visits and service assignments in a wide area, providing for the students an introduction to contemporary complex problems within cross-sections of the community, a study through class work and visits of the structure of society, an overall survey of relief measures coupled with an elementary analysis of the causes of inequality.

Emphasis swung between two objectives, one being the desire to stimulate students intellectually, giving time for more concentrated study with the accompanying satisfaction of growth in discovery, and the other being the practical development of human understanding and skills necessary for mission anywhere.

In 1952 the College Board changed the pattern by placing

more emphasis on the intellectual side. Observation took the place of practical involvement in one situation over the period of a term. Students saw a wider range of activities and were encouraged to analyse the purpose and value of social service within the programme of the Church. After a brief period of exploration and emphasis on the academic approach, the College curriculum stabilised into study, observation and practical involvement in Sunday School, Bible class, hospital visiting and ward services, each student under the direction of a tutor undertaking one weekday and one Sunday assignment, based as before on Preparatory and Evaluation Training Classes.

Students took part in the work of many different parishes, second Year Home Mission students being attached to a specific parish for both Sunday and weekday work under the guidance of the minister and deaconess. They were also linked with both state and voluntary Social Service Agencies. Work was planned in conjunction with the Industrial Organiser of the Home Board, with the Scottish Pastoral Association and the Frontier Group. The original concept of community involvement was stretched to meet the complexity of a post-war world.

Students were attached for work in new housing areas and in industry—'Are you from the police?' inquired an anxious voice as two students made their first contact with the employees of a local laundry. They were given entry to a primary school to conduct a weekly service, to experimental teenage clubs such as the Blue Door where young people come who would never conform to the old pattern of club activity, the Catacomb where they bought coffee and talked, the Old Kirk where at the Youth Club a beat group supplied the music, the Holy Beats who occasionally performed at evening service and Sunday School.

Their work led them to constant re-appraisal of the ministry of the Church within society. There is an account in the later sixties of how they came to the conclusion that they had spent far too much of their leisure time in church buildings and not enough in being actively concerned during their life with ignorance, distrust, tension and human need. In addition to the work already undertaken, contact was made with 'Cephas', a local experiment by five Edinburgh West End churches under the leadership of a staff member of the Church of Scotland Youth Committee. The intention was to provide a centre for young people who remained outside any Church or organised activity; there he was accepted, whether fighting drunk, breaking up the Chapel Service or being imaginatively objectionable. The experience of genuine friendship with no hint of 'being done good to' brought to some the healing, the wholeness, they needed. In the dimly lit basement, with some two hundred teenagers dancing to the deafening electric guitars, the St Colm's helpers shared in this caring community and in the later development of work done by those West End churches.

Reference to a student's practical note-book gives an indication of the varied experience available in the mid-fifties and sixties to any student involved in the study and practice of social work. These note-books gave written reports and evaluation of each visit or activity undertaken by the student and were read by at least two members of staff. Some of the visits paid by this student during the course of two years included visiting men's and women's wards in varying hospitals, Woman's Guild meetings held on Church premises, and Guild Meetings in an incurables' ward where topical programmes included a 'Matter of Opinion' panel on such subjects as Scottish Home Rule, Pay for Nurses, Why do Crooks get off Scot-free?

This student records how she took part in an Intermediate

Youth Club held in converted shop premises where they were busy with a 'Ballet Atom' rehearsal followed by the Epilogue, in a Young Mothers' Hour in a well warmed Session House enjoying films and a travel talk, while the offspring were catered for on the floor above; she visited other women's gatherings where there was plenty of scope for talks and racy discussion on current events.   There was extensive home visiting, especially where mental defectives were housebound.

At the approved school for girls she joined in their talk, played games and responded to their requests for modern records.   She visited a number of social clubs to evaluate conditions, went to a school for handicapped children and had the opportunity also to observe work amongst Girl Guides, Brownies, Wolf Cubs and Life Boys, to partake in a Sunday School picnic and visit an Eventide Home.   In many of these activities the student took some part, but for observation only she went to see such places as the Corporation Welfare Department, a meeting of the Edinburgh Town Council, and two factories.   Another regular form of practical work was that of helping in the Simon Square Centre for the care of handicapped people; some students went to help in a summer holiday for handicapped women.

The carefully planned vacation work continued to take many forms and to expand in variety.   Students went to help with seaside missions and holiday camps, with berry-pickers and fishergirls, with Home Mission stations, with World Council of Churches Camps in France, Italy, Holland, England, Wales, Ireland and Iona, and other work camps and youth camps in Switzerland, Austria, Exeter, South Wales, Dunblane, Skelmorlie and the Ecumenical Institute at Coventry Cathedral, also to Schoolgirl Camps run by the Student Christian Movement.   They joined with New College in campaigns run during the Easter and summer vacations and took part also in the Tell Scotland and Kirk Week activities. From 1953 student teams conducted to Iona, girls from Tynepark Approved School who had been entrusted to their care.

Other vacation activities included study visits to the World Council of Churches Centre at Bossey, to the Kirchentag in Germany, to Holland for the purpose of examining and sharing in Deaconess and Social Welfare work. Two students with the Principal attended the 1961 European Christian Youth Assembly at Lausanne. Two trained teachers decided to work as auxiliary nurses in a hospital, and a Dutch student training to serve in Scotland worked with the Salvation Army in a red light district of Amsterdam.

One year two Foreign Mission students went on a round of visits to various experiments being carried out by the Church as well as by the community. They attended Local Authority Community Associations, a Scottish Rural Women's Institute, a Miners' Institute, a Health Centre, a Church Family Centre and House Church Groups.

These various activities were undertaken alike by Home and Foreign Mission students. The close association of these areas of training for 'Home' or 'Foreign' work was often commented on by visitors to the College, especially those from overseas.

The practical work programme brought contact with varied ages and conditions and was a salutary check to facile optimism as well as a stimulating encounter with neighbourhood reality and ebullient youth.

An Easter Mission

Holy Week and Easter Sunday did not always fall within the College term, but when they did the opportunity was seized to celebrate them not only with prayer and meditation,

but also with involvement and mission.   In the House
Guild Letter of 1948 the question had been asked, 'Might
there not be more opportunity for students in St Colm's to
work alongside men undergoing similar training with a view
to arriving at a deeper understanding of each other's ways?'
This question was answered in the following year by an
invitation from New College Theological students to
co-operate with them in the running of a twelve-day
evangelistic campaign in Alloa at the end of the 1949 spring
term.   This joint venture was carried out in each of the
ensuing three years at Cowdenbeath, Broxburn and
Haddington.   In each campaign the St Colm's students were
associated from the beginning with all the planning and
preparation.   Groups from the two colleges met together
for some weeks beforehand for prayer, discussion of method
and consideration of questions that might be asked in the
campaign area.

St Colm's students were responsible for the children's
meeting, the theme one year being the Lord's Prayer, based
on the events of Holy Week.   Each Bible story was accompanied by a modern parallel.   The effort met with a lively
response and the children paved the way into their homes.

Evaluation of the campaign brought discoveries about the
campaigners and those they visited.   Each group realised
that if they were to work together they must learn to accept
each other in their different ways of interpreting certain
aspects of the faith; they must recognise the danger of
appeal to emotion at the expense of will and reason; they
must realise the temptation when visiting to take the easy
way of reading a text and saying a prayer rather than seeking
relationship.   It was agreed that the aim was not primarily
to get people to become members of the Church, but rather
to help them toward relationship with God, deepening that
which was already there.   One wise suggestion was that

campaigners would have done well beforehand to think out
a brief statement on 'What the Gospel means to me'.   In
the effort to contact young people it was agreed that it
would be more profitable to go where they naturally
congregate instead of expecting their presence at meetings.
Stress was laid upon the importance of including the local
church people in planning and executing the campaign.

Discoveries about those visited included the realisation
that regular Church members had little or no prayer life;
that many who never went to church nevertheless taught
their children to pray.   Lack of contact between denominations was unconsciously illustrated by the householder
who, on finding a missioner on her doorstep said, 'I'm a
Roman Catholic—it's strange you should come today for
this is our Good Friday.'   Her reply led them to share their
faith with each other.

In 1959 the College met to plan the way in which they
should spend Holy Week.   They sought involvement in the
contemporary world and found it through contacting the
New College Missionary Society who worked in Greenside
—an area due for demolition—and who were to be on
vacation during Easter week.   St Colm's were glad to fill
the gap.   Each evening during the week staff and students
set out in twos to visit the old people and shut-ins leaving
them a gift of eggs, symbolic of their desire to share the
gladness of Easter.   Others ran a club for the children and
on Sunday afternoon entertained sixty-seven of them at
St Colm's where they spent most of the time in the garden,
closing with the Easter story in Chapel, a fitting end to a
happy day which had started for the students with a dawn
service on Calton Hill overlooking Greenside, the climax
to a week wherein they had been deeply enriched.

In 1961 a similar programme was based on the St James'
Mission in a district of appalling slums, now no more.

Every day during Holy Week staff and students took part, running an afternoon club for the children and visiting old people.   On Easter Sunday afternoon the children came streaming through the gates of the College for games, tea and brief age-group services in Chapel and Common Room.

CHAPTER NINE

Development in Home Mission

'MISSION is wherever you are'—from the beginning the realistic identification of Church service at home and abroad added enrichment to the College curriculum, those going overseas having direct contact with the problems and opportunities of the Church at home, and those serving in home countries being given a wide knowledge of the church throughout the world. Both groups carried with them into their work an appreciation of other traditions of worship and an awareness of points of growth and experiment within the Church. Both groups treasured the team approach, the unity in College, the gradual realisation of wholeness in Christ. For specific area studies at home or abroad there were separate sessions, but for all participants the concept of the wholeness of mission applied to whatever work they undertook.

The intention of the College from its first days was to offer training to Home Mission as well as to Foreign Mission students, although initially, when accommodation was limited, priority had to be given to women going overseas. Gradually, however, the use of women in Home Mission was developed by the United Free Church of Scotland (as also in the Church of Scotland) and the need for their formal training was acknowledged. In 1908 the College became the recognised place of training for women workers in home mission and from then on Home Mission and Foreign Mission studies in the College ran side by side.

Practical experience in church work for both groups was made increasingly possible through the move to the vicinity of St Bernard's Church in 1909.

The number of fully trained Church Sisters within the United Free Church of Scotland grew steadily and by the time of the Union with the Church of Scotland in 1929 they were about sixty in number. After their own union with the equally numerous Parish Sisters of the Church of Scotland, they continued under the name of Church Sisters until in 1949 all were commissioned as deaconesses, coming within the original Order of Deaconesses of the Church of Scotland, which had been inaugurated in 1887.

In the Irish Presbyterian Church, the Women's Association for Home Missions had been operating since 1908 when a Deaconess House had been established in Belfast under the leadership of Miss Kathleen Rea, a Church of Scotland Deaconess, who also initiated a small training scheme. In 1944 this work, which had been dwindling, was revived through the formation of the Women's Home Mission of the Presbyterian Church. The first Irish candidates for training as Church Sisters were sent in September of that year to St Colm's for the two-year course, and since then all Home Mission students have been trained there as had been overseas candidates since the beginning of the College.

Students attending Home Mission classes at St Colm's might have come from Scotland or Ireland, from the West Indies, Africa or India, with the intention of serving the Church in their own country or going abroad to do work comparable with deaconess work, perhaps with a special concern for women's work. For those serving overseas the course would include study of the Christian Family Year, the Christian Home Movement, Christian festivals and the training of leaders in Church and society.

A succession of members of staff gave outstanding service in the training of women in Home Mission work, each making a typically individual contribution. Between 1946 and 1969 the Home Mission tutor was always a Church Sister or a Deaconess. Two particular stages in the development of Home Mission training, one in the 1940's and another in the 1960's may be examined in more detail.

The study of the human being in his environment—family, housing conditions, work and leisure—was emphasised by Miss Frances Danskin who succeeded Miss Beth Davey in 1946. A study of Trevelyan's *Social History* alongside that of contemporary social services, statutory and voluntary, helped the student to evaluate the present state of society in the context of the past. During district visiting the student realised the value of this practical knowledge of social welfare facilities, while opportunities of observing meetings of the local Council of Social Service gave insight into methods of approach. Although not carrying a caseload, the student had a specific group of people whom she visited regularly, making notes, and reporting back to the seminar on visiting held weekly in College, where she considered her position as a Christian in relation to such issues as birth-control, pre-marital relationships, unmarried mothers and adoption.

The necessity for a third year of training for Home Mission students was expressed by deaconesses at a Women's Home Mission conference in 1960. Deaconesses working in new housing estates felt the need for greater understanding of the situations affecting people in the changing social pattern. The removal to strange surroundings meant the loss of the 'extended family' in the old neighbourhood—grandparents, uncles and aunts—the familiar circle. Women felt lonely and depressed, juvenile delinquency increased.

The first year of the Social Study Course at Glasgow University was thereupon made available to Scottish deaconess students for a few years, until the pressure for admission for students to the full course in Glasgow became too heavy. This year was taken as the first year of deaconess training before proceeding to St Colm's, the students living in the University Settlement with others of many nationalities. They shared classes with men and women training to be probation officers, psychiatric social workers, medical social workers, child care officers, and learned to understand their approach and point of view. They had lectures on psychology, physiology, social administration, social biology, case work and work among old people. Two days each week were taken up with practical work. Although this Glasgow course is no longer available to deaconess students, the need for a third year of training has been accepted by the General Assembly, to be spent in gaining some specialist or wider qualification and various experiments are being made in this direction.

During the 1960's, classes in social studies continued within the College, under the tuition of Miss Charlotte Clunie, and students attended a university class in Social Science one morning a week. The College classes were planned individually, according to previous experience and future need. The study was based on the practical needs of the community and the corresponding services provided by the State, and included such fields as care for mothers, for the sick, the handicapped, the unemployed. Vivid illustrations of social needs and conditions elsewhere were supplied by students from other countries.

Weekly sessions were held for all Home Mission students during the autumn term of their second year, when a group study was made of conditions of work and leisure based on personal experience gained during previous practical work.

There was discussion on such topics as authority, responsibility and job security, supplemented by background reading on the Christian approach to industrial society. Visits were made to a local church industrial group and to a youth employment office where material was supplied relating to the transition from school to work. The management of a local laundry allowed students to speak to employees during the morning break: they made social contact and individual girls from the laundry came to visit them in the College.

Visiting remained an important element, while classes in purpose and method continued as before, emphasising current problems: the elderly, people at 'high risk' such as the recently bereaved, the handicapped, those living alone, the dying. Questions were discussed concerning the nature of illness and anxiety, counselling and pastoral encounter, pastoral availability, the Church as the healing community. Socio-drama was often used to bring to life typical pastoral situations.

Training in Home Mission introduced the student to a fresh conception of her whole ministry and increased her capacity to train others in worship, Bible Study, and youth work in all its branches. Aware of the strategic importance of lay participation, St Colm's taught with repeated emphasis the necessity for leadership training within the congregation. In recent years this has become a regular feature of church policy and is carried out through the formation of groups in a parish, responsible not only for particular church activities but also for neighbourhood work in which the congregation with new insights could be involved, especially by collaborating (as was the experience of the deaconess during her training) with social welfare agencies and movements for local reform.

Particularly effective is the team approach, now in evidence in several areas, where church members are combining with social welfare and health officers as a ministry to serve the whole man, to grapple with live issues of human strife, apathy, despondency, sickness and mental hurt, and to bring health in soul, mind and body. Such group involvement gives to the Deaconess opportunities for service far beyond the limited scope of weekly church routine, and in addition brings to each member of the team an extension of his individual capacity to alleviate misery.

Situations are now emerging where a deaconess may be seconded to specialised community work, employed by the local authority concerned. She may work as a full-time agent for Social and Moral Welfare, or as a co-ordinating link between statutory, voluntary and Church groups in a developing area, or at a Family Advice Centre. By 1970 there were some seventy deaconesses working in Scotland under various auspices, the Church being the largest employer through its Home Board, Youth Committee, Social Service Committee and Moral Welfare Board.

It did not always follow that a deaconess was given full scope when appointed to serve in a parish. Fully aware as she was of the Church's need for comprehensive reform she often found herself circumscribed by outworn custom, frustrated by institutional determinism, and condemned as incapable of doing what was regarded as her job. On the other hand in those situations where freedom has been given for a creative approach with youth and adults there emerges lively involvement, eager commitment, and some degree of successful community achievement, especially where the Team approach already functions.

Plans are now being formulated for the future of the diaconate within the Church of Scotland. Members of St Colm's staff, together with a group drawn from both the Home Board and the Deaconess Board of the Church of Scotland, are thinking through the renewal of the diaconal

E

ministry of the whole Church from the perspective of mission in a global dimension. This renewal and transformation is seen as part of the total renewal of the Church.

A proposal was laid before the General Assembly of 1972 to the effect that the diaconate for both men and women should be recognised as being an integral part of the total ministry of the Church, having therein a distinctive role. The terms of this proposal speak of service to the world in its need, of encouraging and training the laity for such service, of emphasising through involvement the particularly urgent opportunities within the current situation: in short, of enabling the Church the better to fulfil her ministry of diakonia to the world.

CHAPTER TEN

The College Community

LIFE in community was rare in Scotland where so much educational work was non-residential. To the Founders of St Colm's it was a vital issue, an essential experience for the candidate who was preparing to go abroad. Each College generation has made its own experiments and discoveries, and the pattern has emerged according to current need. At the heart of it all lies the challenge whereby individuals with widely varying national and cultural background are called to participate in a setting of community and worship where the gaiety and pain, the friendship and tension, the faith and the fear encountered in the world of mankind are reflected in the daily round of personal dealings one with another.

Difficulties were inevitable—varying ages, nationalities, races, educational achievements, devotional practices, personal routines, and most especially the individualism and determination that so frequently lay behind a person's decision to enter for training. 'There are those who accept the light only if it comes through their own gas meter,' as was once said by Professor T. W. Manson.

It was, of course, this same variation that gave such rich content to College life, and through the common missionary purpose there emerged the life of friendship, exploration and self-discovery that transcended differences. Students experienced that unity of common allegiance which embraces diversity and demands no corporate uniformity. The original intention was to create a natural, free and wholesome family life, governed only by the law of mutual loyalty and service. The House Guild with its annual letter, the student business meetings, debates and conferences, and the social recreation which is a marked feature of the College life served continually to realise this intention.

Student involvement in household affairs was given impetus through the emergence of the House Guild. A letter had come from an old student wishing that she had undergone training in committee procedure. This request fitted in with a growing sense of need for recording the common mind and experience of the College group, and so in October 1898 it was decided to establish the House Guild with the object of providing weekly discussion of subjects of general interest as well as accustoming students to methods of conducting meetings. A Constitution was drafted describing the aim as being the representation of the corporate life of the College and the establishment of a link between present and past students. Meetings were to be held at least three times each term; in addition, to cope with staff and student participation in household matters, a small committee was appointed which met weekly for the reading of the Journal and discussion on domestic affairs. Business was scrupulously conducted in accordance with correct procedure and every opportunity was thus provided in early years for the student body to enjoy an active part in democratic control.

The weekly Journal was written by different students in turn and has been carefully preserved in bound volumes, while an annual House Guild Newsletter in the form of a carefully compiled booklet reports on the year's happenings and gives news of former staff and students to the far-flung membership.

Further involvement in the maintenance of the building was provided through the 'Sections' system by which groups of students with a staff member were responsible for certain house and community duties—care of the Chapel, the Library and so on. Useful experience of public speaking was given through the weekly Reports Class where students were called upon to give an account of their practical work.

Boarders

The many and varied boarders, who were accepted at St Colm's when there were vacancies, are mentioned again and again in the records as enriching the life of the College through bringing first-hand experience of other nationalities, languages, customs and religions. Requests for accommodation frequently came from the British Council, especially for postgraduate botanists, or from the College of Nursing for nurses taking advanced courses. No questions were asked about religion, so amongst overseas students in addition to Christians there were Muslims and Hindus, and amongst the British an assortment of many persuasions, including atheists.

A Ghana postgraduate writes in 1970:

'When I gained admission to do a postgraduate course at Edinburgh University in the Department of Botany I was advised to contact the Principal of St Colm's College. I was very much fascinated by the reply from Miss Jean Fraser. She expressed great joy for my coming to live with them because, she wrote, St Colm's has always been a home for overseas students and she specifically mentioned countries like India, Pakistan, Sierra Leone and even Ghana. In my mind's eye I was trying to envisage my life in St Colm's, and started feeling proud that I was not going to be lonely, that I was going to share such a rich fellowship of people, of different cultures and backgrounds, from different places in the world, unlike my other friends who were going to stay alone with a landlady in Manchester. I felt completely secure.

'The first things that impressed me most on my arrival were the tidiness of the College and its compound; the easy access to members of staff, students and boarders; the way both staff and students and boarders met at table for meals and chatted freely about various topics that cropped up, sharing jokes and some even bursting into loud laughter, affecting people at other tables.

'Throughout my stay in St Colm's I observed that the welfare of each was the concern of the other. I was asked several times, even in a day, how I was getting on with my studies, health, etc.

'I can safely say that I improved my social and spiritual life at St Colm's. I enjoyed doing the dishes and arranging the cups and saucers in the cupboard, and I took active part in the games that were organised in each season. I improved my performance in lawn and table tennis and learned to play croquet. I also made an attempt to learn piano playing.

'At the same time that I was satisfying my social instincts I never neglected my spiritual needs. There were opportunities for this in the College by way of daily evening prayers, Sunday morning worship, communion services, Friday Open House and College Fellowship, and a host of other religious activities.

'Taking part in all these activities reminded me of my schooldays in Ghana when I was an active member of the Christian Fellowship. So, to some extent, my life in St Colm's was a continuation of my life as a student in Ghana. St Colm's is a marvellous family with a close fellowship, unsurpassed by any I have ever experienced.'

An Australian private student describes her reactions:

'St Colm's was primarily a profound experience of people

and living, symbolising enduring reality and validity. From the beginning I saw St Colm's as a training institution characterised by a healthy and I suspect rare unorthodoxy, a unique catholicity in its view of the Church and the world, and an even rarer sensitivity to the needs of the Church and the world as they are manifested in the people being trained to serve both. Here there seemed to co-exist a truly catholic vision of the Church with something of the best Scottish tradition extending back through the Reformation to the rich culture of the Celtic tradition. Through reading and many visits to Iona, I was impressed not only with the language and spirit of the Scots Confession, but even more with the truly whole vision of life and faith encountered there.

'The staff at St Colm's represented a variety of Christian experience, but they held in common a maturity of faith which, with none of the arrogance or rigidity of dogmatism, was sufficiently humble and flexible to accept and confront both the intellectual and practical challenge of change. The catholic character of the College was further manifest in the student and boarder personnel. In a real sense the whole world seemed to converge there, representing a diversity of cultural, occupational and theological background which constituted a source of deep personal enrichment. All the learning and encounters I had had in Europe and England, with the Roman Catholic and Orthodox Churches in particular, seemed to be gathered up and given meaningful focus.'

Men Students at St Colm's

In 1951 the Church of Scotland Foreign Mission Committee decided to give a one-term training to men missionary candidates, this to take place at St Colm's. The Reverend John Fleming, now a lecturer at St Andrews

University, who has served in Manchuria was appointed as Tutor, and the non-residential course was attended by two married couples and four men. This was followed in the autumn term of 1952 by the attendance of five men, two with wives, who lived at No. 5 Inverleith Terrace with their tutor, the Reverend W. Young (now Bishop of Sialkot), but shared the College life throughout the day, enriching the worship and singing, and sharing in Christmas visiting.

By the 1953 autumn term ten men were resident in College and were noted for willing co-operation in Section Duties and College affairs, including host duties on Open Days. Women students joined in parts of their course run under the direction of Dr A. Craig from Kalimpong. The plan was repeated with nine men in 1954 with the Reverend Frank Ryrie as first man to be appointed to the regular staff of St Colm's. The combined groups studied the Theology of Mission with Professor J. S. Stewart and joined for other lectures, but it was felt that lectures had been overdone and that there should be more emphasis on tutorials, directed reading and practical work—this last to include Book-keeping, Visual Aids, Car Maintenance, Health, Care of Buildings and Domestic chores in the life of a missionary.

It had proved impossible to house the men and their wives in the College, but fortunately No. 24 Inverleith Terrace fell vacant and was purchased to be equipped as a family residence by September, 1955, housing nine men, three of whom were married, thus making possible a closer integration of men's and women's work in No. 23.

After the autumn term course the house came to be well used during the spring and summer terms by Swiss Basel and Italian missionaries and candidates. For the autumn of 1956 there were ten men candidates, nine of them married, and use had to be made of a nearby furlough house. By that time it was realised that a one-term course for laymen appointed for work abroad was far too crammed and it was decided that from 1957 they should take the normal year's session, while the one-term course continued for clerics.

Tutorship passed into the hands of the Reverend Kenneth MacKenzie who found St Colm's to be a creative meeting place of groups usually held apart in the church and the world—lay and cleric, men and women, home and overseas, different nations, different denominations. He lists the various Missionary Societies represented—Irish Presbyterian, Basel Mission, London Missionary Society, Danish Missionary Society and Paris Missionary Society. In addition there were residents representing the Waldensian Church, the Methodist Church in Ireland and the Presbyterian Church in the United States. He was impressed with the vocational variety—a carpenter, an engineer, a business manager, a doctor, nurses, teachers and ministers; he was glad, having been involved in Foreign Mission, to become aware in a new way of the Church's great Home Mission with its rich variety both in Ireland and Scotland. St Colm's he found to be a powerful force in reducing departmental barriers as well as exposing its group to 'the surge and thunder of the great forces of our contemporary world-resurgent Hinduism and Buddhism, Communism (international and national), missionary Islam, African nationalism, the Ecumenical Movement and the many Churches in which ex-students are serving.'

Mr MacKenzie describes the 1958-59 course: 'Missionary training seems to be based on Boothby's Law: "Make the most of this; it won't last!" Certainly that is the gospel behind the one-term course—Approach to Other Religions, Policies and Problems in the Church Overseas, Social Anthropology (at the University), Religious Education (Moray House), Methods in Evangelism, Group Bible Study,

Vaccinations and Inoculations, the Christmas Play, Motor Maintenance. The students survive on the assumption that this is nothing to what is coming to them. . . . Whether by the time I had escorted them to the College gate they had all the necessary bees in their bonnets, fire in their bellies, and realism in their souls I just don't know.' He speaks with deepest appreciation of the visiting speakers who coped with aspects of the course quite beyond his ken.

Family life brought reality and joy to the College community—Billy in his blazer with minute St Colm's badge, Elizabeth along with Billy celebrating their second birthdays, both frequent attenders at morning prayers. The next year there were five children; perambulators abounded. The September 1966 records speak of six children—Swiss, Irish and Scottish—and in 1968 there was the proud announcement that all 'our' wives had had babies in February or March, including Mrs Bindi of Sierra Leone whose Andrew was the largest and lustiest of them all. This statement was significantly followed by an account of a new course in Family Planning!

It was not easy at first to incorporate training for men missionaries in a College founded and conducted for women; men qualified for the Ministry or other professions did not expect to have to go through further training. Integration took place gradually as residential opportunities opened up, and the value of work, study and social life together became increasingly enriched, bringing mutual help and under-standing. The name of the College was changed to Church of Scotland St Colm's College, and was officially adopted in January 1961.

The families of St Colm's proved essential to its gaiety and development. One man's point of view is expressed:

'The distinctive thing about St Colm's for those of us who studied there was the unique way in which the academic training was given within a context of community and corporate worship. Everything was not subordinated to academic training, which was nevertheless given its proper but not exalted place in the whole scheme. This did not mean that the academic standards were not maintained. Those of us who had been through universities were well stretched at St Colm's, we looked forward to our lectures and found them stimulating. But, for example, in addition to the lectures we had corporate Bible Study in which we were asked to allow the Bible to speak to our hearts as well as our heads, and to allow our fellows to speak to both in God's name. Again, the whole was comprehended in worship.

'And the whole was seen in ecumenical perspective—it was not simply that we studied the traditions, hymns and forms of worship of other denominations: it was that we were asked to allow Truth to make all theology and practice, even our own, transitional. This was good preparation for service overseas.

'In St Colm's I learned for the first time new methods by which knowledge could be imparted other than by lecturing. We did not only receive lectures on Christian Education—methods of education were used which showed us how they worked in practice and how we might experiment in new means of communicating the faith. In Group Bible Study we varied our methods from term to term.

'As Christmas approached we were encouraged to prepare our own versions of a nativity play. How salutary it was that we, who had written the scenes, were expected to submit our drafts to the ruthless scrutiny of the group. What amusement we had in preparing and rehearsing and what joy in presenting the play. Much we learned of the possibilities that lay in using drama to present the gospel.

'One thing which made us feel part of the College was that we were asked to help in the household chores. There was no theoretical discussion about the relationship between the Christian faith and labour, as part of our training we laboured as Christians, thus making our fellowship closer and our studies more realistic.

'We learned new team and group games on the tennis court, knowing that some day we would have the chance to introduce others to these activities which we had so enjoyed. Badminton we played in a neighbouring Church hall—we were not allowed to put on weight! We were happy at St Colm's. It was not just that, like many others, I met my future wife there!'

Various groups of people have always stayed at St Colm's for periods of different length or have attended Courses—missionaries on furlough, ministers' wives, 'Divinity Dames' from New College, English, Irish and Continental Deaconesses. It is felt that more provision for such could be made. Missionaries have often spoken of the need for some place to come to for rest, re-orientation study and spiritual renewal after a period overseas. Some Continental and African Deaconesses have come for short visits and complete courses. It is helpful for the students to have them in the house sharing in Bible Study, Worship and selected classes.

It was realised by those in charge that St Colm's College had special advantages—of being an integral part of the life of the Church, of being free from an examination system, of being in close touch with Church Committees, Church Offices, the University, Moray House College of Education and other centres of learning, of welcoming visiting missionaries and deaconesses experienced in their work, of enjoying a communal life representing men, women and children of many nations and churches. College was an experience of learning through many channels, but especially through relationships.

Responsibility to the community was realised and carried out as an essential element in training, through study of Social Agencies and Legislation, of Ethics, of Politics, of Education, as well as through involvement in practical youth work and social welfare.   Responsibility towards the Church was expressed in a study of Christian Education, Ecumenical Development, Approach to Other Faiths, the Bible, Worship and the Devotional Life, Field Studies and Evangelism, while with study was linked weekly service through Sunday School and other church activities.

The Reverend Roy Manson at the end of his first year on the staff expressed this alignment of the College with both Society and the Church.   He wrote in 1969:

'One of the outstanding things about St Colms is its international connection, status and content.   In this year alone we have had certainly no less than thirty nationalities either here in person or represented here, and that's not even a careful counting; there could probably be added many more, and we have heard quite a lot and seen quite a lot of these various countries.   Ecumenical too— Presbyterian, Anglican, Methodist, Roman Catholic, Greek Orthodox, Lutheran and various united churches.   And multi-religious — Christian, Hindu, Muslim, Atheist, Communist.

'You cannot come to St Colm's without being challenged, opened up and exposed to the realities of the world in which we live and the responsibilities which are laid upon us as Christians.   Current affairs, social responsibility, racial prejudice, riches and poverty, world health, Christian Aid, Shelter, Simon Square, Cala Sona, Alcoholics Anonymous, Uppsala and World Council of Churches—you name it, we have studied it or listened to it.   From Byzantine Art to Peanuts, from East Asian Hymns and Gregorian Chant to Pop Music, from Ancient Greek Liturgy to Modern

Orthodox Sacramental Theology—it has all happened here, and in the course of this one past year. This may well have been a normal year for St Colm's College, but I would declare that it has been no ordinary year for me or for any of us who have submitted to its disciplines. . . . St Colm's is not only a place of learning—it is a way of life—it is a community of *the Way*.'

It is as a community of the Way that St Colm's has continued from 1894 to the present day. This continuity is fostered by a booklet with names, addresses and birthdays of all former staff and students, issued every few years and sent to all life members of House Guild, and by the Annual House Guild Letter. This community is bound together by the Roll of Honour in chapel, by the cycle of intercession and weekly remembrance of birthdays, and by Reunion and Retreat held annually at St Colm's.

Reunion and Retreat

From the early years an annual reunion of former staff and students has been a characteristic feature of the College. The leadership of each Retreat was in the hands of those wise in the practice of prayer and the devotional life who with the staff guided the meditation and the central acts of worship. In the periods of silence and waiting upon God came refreshment of spirit, serenity through renewed affirmation and re-creation for the days ahead. In preparation for the service of intercession on the Sunday afternoon groups from different areas of work met to share their problems, concerns and joys before gathering in the Chapel for worship, thanksgiving and intercession. In the Service of Holy Communion which followed at night, God's mercy was mediated, and in the receiving of the bread and the wine his promise was confirmed 'Lo, I am with you alway, even unto the end of the world.'

The Retreats after the two world wars were significant for renewed contacts—messages came from Japan, China (North, Central and South), Asia Minor, Manchuria, Switzerland, Holland, Russia and Germany, as well as Australia, Africa, India, Ceylon, Burma and West Indies.

The 1969 Retreat with forty participants in residence and a goodly number by day was typical of the college fellowship—a married couple from Ghana, an exile from Biafra, the college secretary from Ceylon, a Swiss student, Dutch and French orderlies, Scots, English and ten Irish. The theme for meditation was St John 13-15; it was led by Miss Fraser, and on Sunday morning the chapel service was recorded for broadcasting on July 27th. In open forum the group discussed such problems as worship and its relevance today, personal and race relations, conflict and unity, the Irish unrest, health and healing.

Each year the report of this gathering tells of the welcome of the familiar building filled with flowers, of the beauty of the garden, the pleasure of meeting with friends and staff, of seeing again those who had been overseas for a number of years. The experience is summed up in the constantly repeated phrase 'We knew ourselves to be at home.'

Retreat House Guild was important because it gave an opportunity for all to discuss business which was related to the world-wide membership of the College. Reports were given from member groups from England, Ireland and Scotland as well as from countries overseas.

Saturday afternoon tea, generally in the garden, brought together many former students and staff unable to attend for the whole weekend. Through challenging talks by those working at home and overseas all realised afresh the unity of the task to which they were committed.

For those brought up in the reformed tradition these Retreats proved to be a new experience of corporate

worship based on silence and meditation.   Through insight
gained in planning such retreats, characterised by a happy
catholicity in leadership two members of staff in association
with the late Principal of Wilson College, Bombay, the
Reverend John Mackenzie, D.D., initiated during the 1940's
the weekend Prayer Schools in Edinburgh which proved
such an inspiration to those who took part.

Towards the Future

The introductory lecture in September 1970 by the Principal, the Reverend Duncan Finlayson, to present-day students indicates the purpose of the College in this decade. The men and women students represent very varied experience—theology, industry, hairdressing, engineering, seafaring, commerce, education, social service, medicine and the Civil Service—and considerable age range. They have come to St Colm's to prepare for Mission wherever they may be.

The lecture emphasised the mood at the receiving end of Christian witness today and challenged the group to analyse both method and content of their message. Public evangelism was out, generalisations were useless, great words like Mission, Evangelism, Service, Fellowship—even The Church—failed to convey any reality because they had depreciated through facile usage. Yet two central factors denoted the purpose of the College training, namely the one unchanging Gospel of the Son of God; the radically changing world.

'Evangelism must find renewed forms of communication for this challenge which can be summed up in the key words Secularisation, Urbanisation, Industrialisation. Large, complex areas of life are increasingly moving out of religiously oriented control into new forms of motivation where the church is regarded simply as irrelevant—because, as Annie Small had predicted concerning the church of her day, though it seemed outwardly flourishing, yet it was under judgment as being inward-looking, non-mission concerned, non-socially involved.

'In St Colm's, therefore, it is required of us

—that we recover the Biblical doctrine of the Church, namely that the Church exists for Mission, not for self-preservation.

—that we examine what Mission truly is—not to take Jesus to people but to enable men and women to discover that He is already there.

—that we maintain a humble openness based on confidence in the Gospel and readiness to admit that we do not know all the answers, an openness to what is being said by novelists, artists, poets, to the voices of the world, for "the world provides the agenda"; an openness to young people as they speak out with integrity.

—that we have the honesty and courage to face the kind of image people have of us and to commit ourselves through action rather than mere talk.

—that we study the real factors underlying Hunger, Development, Race, Immigration, and come to realise what is meant by Church Unity and spiritual pioneering.

'Now is the time to examine our training as a means of enabling a true "formulation of the Laity", the central concept of Laos, the People of God. Jesus sent out seventy, not into a comfortable world to preach the odd sermon, to talk pious platitudes, but as sheep among wolves—yet they came back victorious.'

Members of Staff 1894-1972

1894–1913	Miss Annie H. Small
1895–1898	Miss Mary Martin
*1898–1931	Miss Kate E. Hammer, M.A.
1910–1916	Miss M. Alice Wyld
1913–1938	Miss Florence Mackenzie, M.A.
1916–1918	Miss Josephine Currie
1919–1920 1924–1939	Miss A. E. Marjorie Moinet, M.A.
1920–1922	Miss Ida M. Jewson, B.A.
*1921–1924	Miss Elizabeth R. Craig
1922–1926	Miss Elizabeth G. K. Hewat, M.A., B.D., PH.D.
1926–1930	Miss Hilda F. Hume, M.A. (Mrs J. H. Phillips)
1930–1937	Miss Catherine B. Chell, B.A.
1931–1952	Miss E. Beryl Harris, N.F.U.
1938–1939	Miss Mary S. Johnstone, M.A.
*1938–1941	Miss Mary I. Shannon, M.A., PH.D.
1939–1951	Miss Helen Macnicol, M.A.
1940–1946	Miss Elizabeth M. Davey, B.A. (Mrs O. Brown)
1946–1948	Miss Marjorie Stewart, B.A.
*1946–1952	Miss Frances Danskin, D.C.S.
*1948–1949 1951–1954	Miss Olive Wyon, D.D.
*1952–1955	Miss Celia Calder, M.A.
1952–1961	Miss Janet Watson, M.A., D.C.S.
1948–1950	Miss Doris M. Arrowsmith, M.A.
*1952–1955	Mrs Isabel Paton Henderson, M.A.

(* *Former students*)

1954–1969	Miss Jean M. Fraser, M.A.
*1955–1971	Miss Effie R. Gray, D.C.S.
*1957–1961	Miss Mary I. Lusk, B.A., B.D., D.C.S. (Mrs F. Levison)
*1961–1963	Miss Katherine C. Grainger, D.C.S.
1954–1957	Reverend Frank Ryrie, M.A., D.D.
1956–1968	Reverend Kenneth McKenzie, M.A.
*1963–1968	Miss Charlotte M. Clunie, D.C.S.
*1968–1969	Miss Charlotte M. Stuart, D.C.S.
*1968–1969	Reverend Roy L. Manson, M.A.
1969–	Reverend Duncan Finlayson, M.A.
1970–	Miss Nancy Allison, B.A., B.D.
1970–	Reverend C. J. F. Watt, M.A.
1971–	Miss Moyra McCallum, M.A., B.D., D.C.S.